# Cambridge Elements ☰

Elements in Philosophy of Law
edited by
George Pavlakos
*University of Glasgow*
Gerald J. Postema
*University of North Carolina at Chapel Hill*
Kenneth M. Ehrenberg
*University of Surrey*
Sally Zhu
*University of Sheffield*

# LEGAL RIGHTS AND MORAL RIGHTS

Matthew H. Kramer
*University of Cambridge*

CAMBRIDGE
UNIVERSITY PRESS

# CAMBRIDGE
## UNIVERSITY PRESS

Shaftesbury Road, Cambridge CB2 8EA, United Kingdom

One Liberty Plaza, 20th Floor, New York, NY 10006, USA

477 Williamstown Road, Port Melbourne, VIC 3207, Australia

314–321, 3rd Floor, Plot 3, Splendor Forum, Jasola District Centre,
New Delhi – 110025, India

103 Penang Road, #05–06/07, Visioncrest Commercial, Singapore 238467

Cambridge University Press is part of Cambridge University Press & Assessment,
a department of the University of Cambridge.

We share the University's mission to contribute to society through the pursuit of
education, learning and research at the highest international levels of excellence.

www.cambridge.org
Information on this title: www.cambridge.org/9781009571678

DOI: 10.1017/9781009022293

First published 2025

*A catalogue record for this publication is available from the British Library*

ISBN 978-1-009-57167-8 Hardback
ISBN 978-1-009-01116-7 Paperback
ISSN 2631-5815 (online)
ISSN 2631-5807 (print)

Cambridge University Press & Assessment has no responsibility for the persistence
or accuracy of URLs for external or third-party internet websites referred to in this
publication and does not guarantee that any content on such websites is, or will
remain, accurate or appropriate.

# Legal Rights and Moral Rights

Elements in Philosophy of Law

DOI: 10.1017/9781009022293
First published online: January 2025

Matthew H. Kramer
*University of Cambridge*
**Author for correspondence**: Matthew H. Kramer, mhk11@cam.ac.uk

**Abstract:** In a short span, this Elements volume will delineate the general nature of legal and moral rights and the general nature of the holding of rights, and it will also sketch the justificatory foundations of rights. Hence, it will treat of some major topics within legal, political, and moral philosophy as it combines analytical theses and ethical theses in a complex pattern.

**Keywords:** legal rights, moral rights, legal liberties, legal powers, justice

ISBNs: 9781009571678 (HB), 9781009011167 (PB), 9781009022293 (OC)
ISSNs: 2631-5815 (online), 2631-5807 (print)

# Contents

In a short span, this Elements volume will delineate the general nature of legal and moral rights and the general nature of the holding of rights, and it will also sketch the justificatory foundations of rights. Hence, it will treat of some major topics within legal, political, and moral philosophy as it combines analytical theses and ethical theses in a complex pattern.

## 1 The Hohfeldian Analysis

We can best begin with the schema for analyzing legal relationships that was propounded in the second decade of the twentieth century by the American legal theorist Wesley Hohfeld.[1] His analytical framework has been hugely influential not only in legal and political and moral philosophy but also in several other areas of philosophy (including formal logic) and in some of the social sciences. The basic structure of that framework is encapsulated in Table 1.

**Table 1** Hohfeldian table of legal positions

| ENTITLEMENTS | claim-right (or claim) | liberty | power | immunity |
|---|---|---|---|---|
| CORRELATES | duty | no-right | liability | disability |
| | *First-Order Positions* | | *Higher-Order Positions* | |

To each of the four positions in the upper half of Hohfeld's table, the overarching term "entitlement" applies. Hohfeld himself revealed that, in everyday discourse and in juristic discourse, the noun "right" is very frequently employed to denote each of the positions in the upper half of the table. Indeed, one of his principal concerns was to disambiguate that noun by distinguishing carefully among the four types of entitlements to which it is commonly affixed.

Each of the four entitlements in Hohfeld's table is correlated with the position directly below it. A logical relationship of correlativity between the two positions in each column of the table is a relationship of biconditional entailment. That is, any instance of an entitlement with some specified content entails an instance of the position directly below it with the same content, and vice versa. For example, "John has a legal claim-right vis-à-vis Mary to be paid £100 by her" entails "Mary owes John a legal duty to pay him £100," and vice versa.

As important as the logical relationship of correlativity within each column are the logical relationships between the positions diagonally across from each other on the left-hand half of Hohfeld's matrix, and the logical relationships

---

[1] For a thorough exposition of the Hohfeldian analytical framework, with sustained arguments in support of what I assert in the present section of this Elements volume (and with attention to numerous other major aspects of the framework that cannot even be touched upon here), see Chapters 2 and 3 of Kramer (2024).

between the positions diagonally across from each other on the right-hand half. Duties and liberties are logical duals, just as are claim-rights and no-rights. For example, "Mary owes John a legal duty to pay him £100" is the negation of "Mary is legally at liberty vis-à-vis John not to pay him £100," and vice versa.[2] Liabilities and immunities are logical contradictories, just as are powers and disabilities. For example, "John is legally liable to undergo some specified change in his legal positions through the performance of an action A by Susan" is the negation of "John is legally immune from undergoing the specified change through the performance of A by Susan."

Although these logical relations may seem rather abstruse when they are recounted so laconically, they are what endow the Hohfeldian schema with its immense value in clarifying and analyzing the legal positions which people occupy vis-à-vis one another. Let us very briefly probe each of the four entitlements along with each correlative position. A claim-right is a position of deontic protectedness; when someone holds a claim-right, a typically beneficial aspect of his or her situation is deontically protected. The deontic protection consists in rendering impermissible any interference or uncooperativeness that is at variance with the content of the claim-right. Both the notion of interference and the notion of uncooperativeness are to be understood very broadly here. Interference occurs whenever there befalls some event that worsens the situation of somebody in any way, and uncooperativeness occurs whenever there does not befall some event that would have improved the situation of somebody in any way. Although countless types of interference or uncooperativeness can be legally permissible, any type that falls within the protective ambit of a legal claim-right is legally impermissible.

Correlative to any claim-right held by some party X vis-à-vis some party Y is a duty with the same content, owed to X by Y. A legal duty is a requirement that makes some kind(s) of interference or uncooperativeness legally impermissible. In other words, some kind of noninterference or cooperativeness is rendered legally mandatory by the existence of any legal duty. Except in circumstances where a legal duty is wholly unenforceable, a bearer of a legal duty is legally accountable for the fulfillment of that duty.

A Hohfeldian liberty is an instance of permissibility. When somebody is legally at liberty to φ, the applicable laws permit her to φ. Accordingly, she is not under a legal duty to refrain from φ-ing. A legal liberty is an instance of

---

[2] Each of these propositions is true if and only if the other is false. Each proposition is the negation of the other, and the content of the deontic predicate (that is, the content of the duty or liberty) in each proposition is the negation of the content of the deontic predicate in the other proposition. These twofold instances of negation – the negation at the level of the proposition and the negation at the level of the predicated content, which are often characterized as external negation and internal negation – are characteristic of logical duals.

freedom, but the freedom is deontic rather than modal; it consists in someone's being legally allowed to φ, rather than in her being able to φ. Of course, very often somebody is able to do what she is legally permitted to do. In many other cases, however, her legal liberty to φ is not accompanied by any ability of hers to φ. Conversely, very often someone is capable of doing things which she is not legally at liberty to do.

In the realm of law, the Hohfeldian neologism "no-right" designates a legal position that is correlated with a legal liberty. Any two such correlated positions make up a liberty/no-right relationship that obtains between some specified parties with a specified content. That is, if a liberty and a no-right are indeed correlated, the content of each of them is the same as the content of the other (and the parties between whom either of them obtains are transposedly the same as the parties between whom the other one of them obtains). A no-right in a legal relationship of that kind is a position of rightlessness or unprotectedness. A party P who bears a legal no-right with regard to any act of φ-ing by some other party Q is not legally protected against Q's φ-ing, which will therefore not legally wrong P.

A legal power in the Hohfeldian sense is an ability to effect changes, through one's actions, in one's own legal positions or in the legal positions of other people. A legal liability in the Hohfeldian sense is a position of susceptibility to the undergoing of changes in one's legal positions brought about through the exercise of a legal power by oneself or by somebody else. Powers and liabilities are higher-order legal positions in that their contents always presuppose the existence of other legal positions. By contrast, the contents of many legal claim-rights and many legal liberties do not presuppose the existence of any other legal positions.

Also higher-order positions are legal immunities and legal disabilities. If a person P holds an immunity vis-à-vis another person Q in regard to the modification of some legal position of P through the performance of some specified action(s) by Q, then P is insusceptible to undergoing that modification of his or her legal position through Q's performance of the specified action(s). As is evident, then, an immunity is the negation of a liability. P is immune from the modifying of his or her legal positions through Q's performance of some specified action(s) if and only if P is not liable to undergo any such modifying of those positions through the performance of the action (s) by Q. A disability is a position of powerlessness within the scope of its correlative immunity. In the example just broached, Q bears a legal disability vis-à-vis P with regard to the modifying of P's legal positions through Q's performance of any specified action(s). If Q attempts to modify those legal positions by performing the specified action(s), the attempt will be unavailing. Hence, just as an immunity is the negation of a liability with the same content, so too a disability is the negation of a power with the same content.

Hohfeld was concerned to emphasize not only the biconditional entailment between the two positions in each column of his schema, but also the lack of any biconditional entailment between an entitlement in any one column and an entitlement in any of the other columns. Indeed, the absence of such entailments between the types of entitlements is what he strove to highlight through his efforts to disambiguate the language of "rights." All instances of legal claim-rights and legal liberties are commonly designated as "rights," and many instances of legal powers and legal immunities are commonly so designated. Jurists and legal scholars and ordinary people have therefore frequently been led into paralogisms, as their premises about rights are focused entirely on entitlements of one kind and as the conclusions which they draw from those premises are focused on entitlements of some other kind(s). Hohfeld adduced many examples of such confusion. In response, he and others influenced by his analytical matrix have time and again emphasized the logical disseverability of entitlements in any one column of the matrix from entitlements in any other column thereof. Thus, for example, the holding of a legal claim-right by Mary against being prevented from $\varphi$-ing does not entail her holding of a legal liberty to $\varphi$. Mary can hold a legal claim-right vis-à-vis John that requires him not to prevent her $\varphi$-ing, even while she owes him a legal duty not to $\varphi$ (a duty correlated with a legal claim-right held by him, of course). Because this combination of legal relationships can initially strike some people as unfathomable – as can certain other combinations of legal relationships – Hohfeldian philosophers have essayed to dispel the appearance of oddity by bringing to bear the Hohfeldian categories in a rigorous fashion to show that such combinations are in fact possible.

At the same time, the exponents of Hohfeld's analysis can aptly underscore the closeness of the connections between certain types of Hohfeldian entitlements and other such types. Some links among Hohfeldian entitlements, indeed, are matters of metaphysical or conceptual necessity. For example, the abilities of people to exercise their legal liberties are deontically protected to quite considerable degrees by their elementary legal claim-rights against being subjected to major modes of mistreatment. The fact that people hold those elementary legal claim-rights is hardly a coincidence or an accident. Rather, as H.L.A. Hart contended in Chapter 9 of *The Concept of Law*, all or most people within the jurisdiction of any functional system of governance will hold such legal claim-rights (Hart 1994, 193–200; Kramer 2018, 164–172). No such system could endure more than fleetingly if it failed to impose and effectuate the legal duties that are the correlates of those claim-rights, since the effectuation of such duties is essential for the very cohesiveness of any society. As Hart submitted, the indispensability of those duties and their correlative claim-rights for the sustainability of any system of governance is due to some fundamental features of human beings and of the world in which they live. In other words, it is due to the nature of human beings or to the nature of the human condition. Hart himself characterized the indispensability of those elementary legal duties and their correlative claim-rights as a matter of "natural necessity," but in the parlance of contemporary philosophy it is best characterized as a matter of metaphysical necessity. It is something which follows from the fact that human beings are as they everywhere are. As a matter of metaphysical necessity, then, all or most people within the jurisdiction of any functional system of governance hold legal claim-rights that are conferred upon them by the laws of the system which proscribe major forms of misconduct. Now, given that those claim-rights deontically protect the abilities of people to exercise their legal liberties, and given that the universal or very widespread holding of those claim-rights under any functional system of governance is a matter of metaphysical necessity, what is also a matter of metaphysical necessity is the fact that the abilities of people to exercise their legal liberties are deontically protected by elementary legal claim-rights which they hold. Legal liberties exist as such only when a functional system of governance is in existence, and as a matter of metaphysical necessity a functional system of governance is in existence only when the legal liberties of all or most people in the jurisdiction are accompanied by legal claim-rights that significantly protect the abilities of the holders of those liberties to exercise them. Hence, far from being fortuitous, the accompaniment of legal liberties by legal claim-rights in every jurisdiction is intrinsic to the human condition.

Even tighter are the connections between certain immunities and other entitlements. For example, if Melanie ostensibly has a legal claim-right against being punched in the face by Luke, and if she does not hold any legal immunity against being divested of that claim-right through Luke's clenching of his fist or through his movement of his arm toward her face, we shall have to conclude that she does not genuinely hold such a legal claim-right at all. Given that in those circumstances Melanie can be deprived of her legal claim-right by precisely the sorts of movements of Luke's body that would be involved in his contravening the claim-right, her legal protection against being punched in the face by Luke is then indistinguishable from her not having any legal protection against such misconduct by him. Consequently, the very existence of her claim-right is dependent on its being accompanied by certain legal immunities against the extinguishing of that claim-right. Similarly, if Melanie ostensibly holds a legal liberty vis-à-vis everyone else to walk down Grange Road in Cambridge at noon on any weekday, and if she does not hold any legal immunity (vis-à-vis herself) against being divested of that liberty through her own action of walking down Grange Road at noon on a weekday, we shall have to conclude that she does not really hold such a legal liberty at all. Because in those circumstances Melanie is liable to lose her legal liberty through precisely the sorts of movements of her own body that would constitute her exercising of that liberty, her being entitled to walk down Grange Road at noon on a weekday is then indistinguishable from her not being so entitled. Consequently, the very existence of her legal liberty is dependent on its being conjoined with certain legal immunities (held vis-à-vis herself) against the extinguishing of that liberty.

## 2 What Does the Holding of a Claim-Right Involve?

A key question not answered by Hohfeld's table of legal relationships is the matter of identifying the holders of claim-rights correlative to specified duties. What is the criterion on which we should rely? To see the need for addressing that question, we should mull over the following two legal duties imposed by the system of governance in some (imaginary) country. First, every adult in the jurisdiction below the age of 65 with an income above a specified level is legally obligated to pay at least $5,000 per annum to each parent who is still alive. Second, every adult in the jurisdiction is legally obligated to report his or her parents to a domestic-surveillance agency whenever the parents utter any sentiments of dissatisfaction about the prevailing system of governance. John, a high-income citizen of the country in question, is thus under a legal duty to pay at least $5,000 every year to each of his parents and is also under a legal duty to inform upon either of his parents if either of them evinces any sense of unhappiness about the presiding system of governance. Does each of John's parents hold a legal claim-right correlative to either of his duties? With regard to the first of John's duties, the answer to this question is affirmative. John owes each of his parents a legal duty to pay each of them at least $5,000 per annum. Each parent holds a legal claim-right, vis-à-vis John, to be paid at least $5,000 by him. In regard to the second of John's legal duties, however, the answer to the question just posed is negative. Neither parent holds a legal claim-right to be informed upon by John to a domestic-surveillance agency. John's duty to disclose any recalcitrant utterances by the parents is owed to the prevailing system of governance and more specifically to the surveillance agency, but it is not owed to either of the parents or to anyone else.

At a pre-theoretical level – the level of everyday "common sense" – these conclusions about claim-rights held or not held by John's parents are quite straightforward. However, a philosophical exposition has to go beyond a pre-theoretical level. What is required is a richly theoretical account of the conditions under which a party holds a claim-right correlative to some specified duty. Efforts by philosophers to provide such an account have led to the emergence of two main competing models of what the holding of a claim-right involves: the Interest Theory and the Will Theory.[3] Although each of those theories exists in many different versions that are inconsistent with one another, the best formulation of the Interest Theory is as follows:

> **Interest Theory of Right-Holding**: Individually necessary and jointly sufficient for the holding of a claim-right by $X$ are (1) the fact that the duty correlative to the claim-right deontically and inherently protects some aspect of $X$'s situation that on balance is typically beneficial for a being like $X$, and (2) the fact that $X$ is a member of the class of potential holders of claim-rights.

Several elements of this formulation are in need of elucidation. Let us begin with the phrase "and inherently." Such phrasing indicates that the content of a specified duty D cannot come to pass – and therefore that D cannot be fulfilled – without affecting $X$'s situation in some way that is on balance typically beneficial for beings like $X$. In other words, the reference to the inherency of the deontic protection bestowed by D on some typically beneficial aspect of $X$'s situation is meant to differentiate between protective effects that are fortuitous or incidental and protective effects that are always occurrent through the realization of what D requires. Note that the protection, rather than the derivation of some benefit from the protection, is what is inherent to the satisfaction of the duty; the protection conferred by D on the situation of the holder of a correlative claim-right is typically beneficial for anyone like that holder but is not invariably so.

The protection conferred by a legal or moral duty-not-to-φ is deontic rather than physical or modal. It consists in the fact that φ-ing is made legally or morally wrong by the existence of the duty, rather than in the fact (if it is a fact) that φ-ing has been prevented. Of course, a legal duty or even a moral duty might be given effect through anticipatory measures of enforcement which do prevent any occurrence that is contrary to the content of the duty. However, the undertaking of such anticipatory measures is wholly contingent and is not inseparable from the existence of the specified duty. (Even when legal duties are well enforced, the enforcement typically consists in the imposition of sanctions *ex post* rather than in the performance of preventative actions *ex ante*.) A legal or moral duty in itself – that is, in abstraction from any

---

[3] Some philosophers have essayed to develop alternatives to the Interest Theory and the Will Theory. Most notable are the efforts by Gopal Sreenivasan (2005, 2010) and Mark McBride (2022) to elaborate hybrid theories that combine elements of the Interest Theory and Will Theory. For a piquant variant of the Interest Theory, see Cruft (2019, 11–86); and for a piquant variant of the Will Theory, see Gilbert (2018).

processes of enforcement that might accompany it – does not prevent actions or other occurrences that are at odds with what it requires. Instead, it establishes that any such actions or occurrences are legally or morally impermissible.

Also in need of elucidation is the phrase "on balance is typically beneficial." Because nearly every feature of a person's situation is typically beneficial in some respect or another even when that feature is typically detrimental on the whole, the evaluations essential for applying the Interest Theory to various situations are about what is beneficial or detrimental on balance. Were those evaluations instead about what is beneficial in some respect or another, they would be almost entirely undiscriminating. As for the qualifying adverb "typically" appended to "beneficial," it too is indispensable for the Interest Theory. As has already been mentioned, the aspects of people's situations inherently protected by the holding of claim-rights can be detrimental on balance in exceptional cases even though they are beneficial on balance in the preponderance of cases. Thus, although one's holding of a claim-right always bestows deontic protection on some aspect of one's situation that is normally beneficial on balance, the aspect that is inherently protected is not always beneficial on balance; it is usually beneficial on balance rather than invariably so.

## 2.1 The Evaluative Premises of the Interest Theory: Objectivity

As is manifest, any application of the Interest Theory to this or that set of circumstances must draw upon evaluative premises in order to differentiate between the generally beneficial aspects and the generally detrimental or neutral aspects of people's situations. Having elsewhere expatiated on those premises (Kramer 2024, 181–187), I can here make only a few brief comments. First, the evaluative premises are predominantly objective rather than predominantly subjective. They are predominantly objective in that they ascribe typical on-balance advantageousness or typical on-balance disadvantageousness to various aspects of people's situations irrespective of anyone's beliefs about those aspects or anyone's attitudes thereto. When Interest Theorists gauge whether sundry features of people's situations are typically beneficial on balance or typically detrimental on balance, most of the assessments are not accommodatingly individualized to match the outlook of each person. Still, although the evaluative premises of the Interest Theory of right-holding are preponderantly objective, there is a subjective dimension. Notwithstanding that multitudinous aspects of people's situations are evaluated by proponents of the Interest Theory in an objectively unaccommodating manner as typically beneficial on balance or typically detrimental on balance, one possible aspect of the situation of anyone resides in attaining what he or she keenly desires. That aspect is typically beneficial on balance for a person, even though it is of course not always beneficial on balance.

Hence, for example, somebody who masochistically yearns to be subjected to a specific type of torture can benefit on balance from being subjected to such torture. If a masochistic person Damian enters into a contract that legally obligates his contractual partner Gregory to subject Damian to the specified type of torture – and if the law of the jurisdiction countenances such a contract as a binding agreement instead of invalidating it on grounds of public policy – the aspect of Damian's situation inherently protected by Gregory's contractual duty is the subjection of Damian to the specified type of torture in accordance with his desires. Precisely because the subjection of Damian to torture is indeed in accordance with his deeply felt desires, it is an aspect of his situation that is beneficial on balance for somebody like him even though subjection to torture would be detrimental on balance for just about any non-masochistic person. Consequently, we can correctly conclude that Damian holds a legal claim-right to be subjected to the preferred type of torture by Gregory, who is of course under a legal duty correlative to that claim-right.

What should be noted here is that this subjective element in the evaluative premises of the Interest Theory of right-holding is itself specified objectively. One of those premises is that the realization of the desires intensely felt by a sane person is typically beneficial on balance for anyone like that person. Such a premise is not dependent on the beliefs of any particular individual about the goodness of realizing his or her keenly held desires, nor is it dependent on the higher-order conative attitudes of any individual toward the realization of his or her intense desires. Accordingly, even when the evaluative underpinnings of the Interest Theory accommodate some of the idiosyncrasies of people, those under-pinnings remain objective – for the accommodation is objectively specified.

## 2.2 Evaluative Premises of the Interest Theory: Generality

The set of evaluative assumptions informing any application of the Interest Theory will be thin and general rather than thick and concrete. For example, those assumptions will not enable us to say whether being skillful in the sport of basketball is better than being skillful in the activity of chess, nor will they tell us whether earning a lofty salary in a stressful and regimented line of work is better than earning a moderate salary in a relaxed and flexible line of work. Concrete evaluative matters of those sorts are not addressed in any satisfactory account of the holding of claim-rights. Rather, the judgments about the typical on-balance advantageousness or disadvantageousness of myriad aspects of people's situations are pitched at much higher levels of generality.

Whenever the Interest Theory is marshaled by someone who is seeking to identify the holder of a claim-right, the relevant comparison − at the very high levels of generality just mentioned − is between a party's situation with a certain feature present and a party's situation with that same feature absent. If the presence of that feature will typically improve the situation of the party on balance or will typically avert a worsening of the party's situation on balance, then the feature is of a kind that is inherently protectable by a legal duty and its correlative legal claim-right. Fine-grained evaluative judgments like those broached in my last paragraph above (involving comparisons between different pastimes, for example, or between different detailed ways of life) are beside the point in applications of the Interest Theory. No such detailed judgments are needed, and no such judgments would be pertinent.

## 2.3 The Interest Theory Applied to John's Duties

Let us now consider how the Interest Theory handles the two duties incumbent on John that pertain to his parents (discussed in the opening paragraph of Section 2). Whereas the first of those duties requires John to pay each of his parents at least $5,000 per annum, the second duty requires John to report his parents to a domestic-surveillance agency in the event that they give voice to any seditious sentiments. While one's being paid at least $5,000 per annum is an aspect of one's situation that is typically advantageous on balance, one's being informed upon to a domestic-surveillance agency for one's utterance of disloyal attitudes is an aspect of one's situation that is typically detrimental on balance. Hence, the Interest Theory generates the conclusion that each parent of John is a holder of a legal claim-right correlated with his legal duty to pay each of them at least $5,000 annually. Conversely, the Interest Theory generates the conclusion that neither parent of John holds a claim-right correlated with his legal duty to apprise the domestic-surveillance agency of any dissentient utterances by the parents. Each of these verdicts tallies with any credible pre-theoretical understanding of the legal relationships between John and his parents, and each verdict is indeed perfectly straightforward. Moreover, as will shortly be seen, the same conclusions are also reachable by the main rival to the Interest Theory: the Will Theory.

Nonetheless, although the Interest Theory as applied to the circumstances of John and his parents is a ratification of common sense, there are many other circumstances where common sense provides very little guidance or unreliable guidance. In regard to such circumstances, the Interest Theory furnishes reliable guidance that is grounded on a richly theoretical understanding of the phenomenon of right-holding rather than on ad hoc propensities. Furthermore, although the Interest Theory of right-holding as applied to the scenario of John and his parents is in accordance with the Will Theory of right-holding as applied to that scenario, the convergence is at the level of their bottom-line conclusions rather than at the level of their justifications for those conclusions. Besides, even at the level of bottom-line conclusions, the two theories diverge in application to manifold other sets of circumstances. We can readily see as much by turning now to the Will Theory.[4]

## 2.4 The Will Theory of Right-Holding

Like the Interest Theory, the Will Theory has been propounded in diverse forms by its sundry exponents. Nevertheless, the versions of the theory overlap sufficiently to warrant the following formulation of the gist of the Will Theorists' position:

> **Will Theory:** Both necessary and sufficient for $X$'s holding of a claim-right correlative to some specified duty is that $X$ is competent and authorized to control the existence and enforcement of that duty.

This formulation of the Will Theory is in need of some elucidation and amplification. Straightaway, however, the inconsistencies between the Will Theory and the Interest Theory should be palpable. Although the extension of the Will Theory's criterion overlaps considerably with that of the Interest Theory's criterion, the two theories generate divergent conclusions in quite a few cases. Their extensional overlap falls well short of extensional equivalence. Even more clearly, the two theories diverge intensionally. Conditions singled out by either theory as necessary and sufficient for the holding of a claim-right are markedly different from those singled out by the rival theory.

In my articulation of the Will Theory, the notion of competence refers to the basic mental and physical abilities through which a party can make the sorts of choices that are involved in controlling the existence and enforcement of a specified duty. A party who lacks those abilities is not capable of holding claim-rights, by the reckoning of the Will Theorists. (We shall return to the matter of competence shortly.) The notion of authorization in my formulation of the Will Theory refers to the fact that a party is endowed with the Hohfeldian powers through which the existence and enforcement of a specified duty can be controlled. Such powers will have had to be conferred upon a party by some relevant law(s) or by some relevant moral principle(s), if that party is to qualify as a holder of a legal or moral claim-right that is correlated with the legal or

---

[4] The Interest Theory of right-holding has been subjected to a number of criticisms over the past few decades. In Kramer (2024, 187–208), I ponder and rebut all the main such criticisms.

moral duty to which the powers pertain. Or so the Will Theorists insist. Hence, those theorists are submitting that any holder of a claim-right CR is possessed of Hohfeldian powers to control the existence and enforcement of the duty which is correlated with CR, and that any holder of CR is endowed with sufficient cognitive and physical abilities to make choices between exercising and not exercising those Hohfeldian powers. Intellectual abilities and normative abilities are constitutive of the holding of claim-rights, according to the Will Theorists.

Further elucidation of the central tenet of the Will Theory can best proceed through some amplification. We need to fathom what is involved in the controlling of a duty through the exercising of Hohfeldian powers. On this point, Hart – the pre-eminent champion of the Will Theory in the twentieth century – valuably shed some light. He differentiated among three main stages at which the powers of control are held: the pre-violation stage, the post-violation stage, and the post-judgment stage (1982, 183–184). At each of these junctures, the Will Theorists contend, a holder of a claim-right possesses two relevant Hohfeldian powers through which the holder can exercise control over a duty. For most duties, the first of the three stages is the only one that is ever reached. That is, because most duties go unviolated, there do not arise any occasions for legal proceedings or other measures through which those duties are enforced and any violations are rectified. Hence, the pre-violation phase of a duty's existence is the sole phase for most duties, and it is of course the stage in which *every* actual duty exists (perhaps for an indefinite duration) at some time or another. At that pre-violation juncture, by the reckoning of the Will Theory, the holder of a claim-right correlative to a specified duty is endowed with a Hohfeldian power to keep the duty in existence and with a Hohfeldian power to extinguish the duty.

Subsequent stages of control over a duty materialize only when the duty in question has been contravened. At the post-violation juncture, according to the Will Theory, the holder of a claim-right correlative to a specified duty is endowed with a Hohfeldian power to waive any enforcement of the duty and with a Hohfeldian power to initiate and pursue such enforcement. (Each of the powers mentioned here can in fact be a set of multiple powers.) If the party who holds the claim-right does exercise his or her power to effectuate the duty by going ahead with a process of enforcement, and if that process is pursued successfully, it will lead to a prescribed remedy. The Will Theorists submit that, at the post-judgment stage where a remedy has been prescribed, the holder of a claim-right correlative to the contravened duty is endowed with a Hohfeldian power to insist upon the implementation of the remedy and with a Hohfeldian power to waive the implementation of the remedy. At each of the three stages delineated by Hart, then, a holder of a claim-right correlative to a specified duty – as envisioned by the Will Theory – is endowed with a pair of Hohfeldian powers (or a pair of sets of Hohfeldian powers) through which the existence or effectuation of the duty can be controlled. Although many a duty will never go beyond the first of those three stages, a party is not a holder of a claim-right correlative to a given duty unless he or she would hold the Hohfeldian powers of control over that duty at each stage that might arise. Such is the conception of right-holding advanced by the Will Theory. Hart famously distilled the pith of that theory as follows: "The idea is that of one individual being given by the law exclusive control, more or less extensive, over another person's duty so that in the area of conduct covered by that duty the individual who has the right is a small-scale sovereign to whom the duty is owed" (1982, 183).

### 2.4.1 Powerful but Question-Begging Objections to the Will Theory

The most common objections to the Will Theory of right-holding within the philosophical literature are question-begging in that they presuppose the fallaciousness of the main tenet of the Will Theory while endeavoring to refute that tenet. Now, to acknowledge the question-begging character of those objections is scarcely to suggest that they are misguided or weak. On the contrary, every one of them is a telling indictment of the shortcomings of the Will Theory. Admittedly, because they beg the question against the Will Theory, they will generally be ineffective in convincing the proponents of that theory to repudiate it. Nevertheless, for anyone not already enamored of the Will Theory, the following criticisms will stand as formidable reasons to eschew its account of the holding of claim-rights.[5]

First, according to the Will Theory, nobody can ever hold a claim-right against being murdered by anyone else. Likewise, nobody can ever hold a claim-right against being subjected to a violent attack that will leave him or her permanently comatose. By the lights of the Will Theorists, the notion of a claim-right not to be murdered or a claim-right not to be rendered comatose is unsustainable. No one can ever hold a claim-right with such a content – by the lights of those theorists – because anybody who is a victim of a murder or of a coma-inducing attack will be incompetent to exercise any Hohfeldian powers at the second and third stages of the existence of the contravened duty. Thus, the Will Theorists are committed to concluding that a murderous or coma-inducing attack does not violate any legal or moral claim-rights of its victim. They are similarly committed to denying that a legal or moral duty to abstain from such an extreme crime is ever owed by a potential perpetrator to any potential victim of the crime.

---

[5] For a much more detailed exposition of these criticisms, see Kramer (2024, 257–268).

Second, Hart's insistence that individuals do not hold any claim-rights against being murdered or rendered comatose was partly an offshoot of his broader insistence that the institutions of criminal law do not bestow any legal claim-rights upon individuals or groups. Hart observed correctly that a victim of a crime does not hold the pairs of Hohfeldian powers which would have enabled the victim to control the existence and enforcement of the legal duty that has been breached by the perpetration of the crime. As Hart wrote: "A person protected only by the criminal law has no power to release anyone from its duties, and though, as in England, he may in theory be entitled to prosecute along with any other member of the public he has no unique power to determine whether the duties of the criminal law should be enforced or not" (1982, 184). Indeed, Hart here understated the matter. Not only does a person protected by criminal-law prohibitions have no legal powers to *waive* most of the duties imposed by those prohibitions, but in addition such a person has no legal powers to *keep* the duties in existence. Those legal duties persist not because of any actions performed by such a person, but instead because of legal immunities which accompany the duties and which prevent them from being extinguished. At the post-violation stage, moreover, the vast majority of criminal-law proceedings in a country such as England are pursued by public prosecutors rather than by the individuals who have been the victims of crimes. It is the prosecutors rather than the victims who hold the relevant Hohfeldian powers. Furthermore, the rare prosecutions that are pursued privately in England cannot usually go ahead without the assent of the Director of Public Prosecutions. At the post-violation stage, then, a victim of a crime is decidedly not furnished with sovereign control over the enforcement of the duty that has been contravened by the perpetrator of the crime. Similarly, at the post-judgment stage, a victim of a crime in a jurisdiction such as England typically does not have any Hohfeldian powers to determine whether the sentence pronounced by the judge will be implemented or not. In short, at none of the three stages outlined by Hart – much less at each of the three stages – do potential victims of crimes in most jurisdictions possess Hohfeldian powers of control over the duties incumbent on potential malefactors. Consequently, by the reckoning of Will Theorists such as Hart, the criminal-law prohibitions in most jurisdictions do not confer any legal claim-rights upon the parties who might be victimized by transgressions of those prohibitions. No such claim-rights are held by individuals under the criminal law of most jurisdictions, or so the Will Theorists insist.

Third, under most minimum-wage laws – which require employers to pay their workers at or above some specified per-hour levels of remuneration – prospective employees are not legally empowered to waive the duties owed by the employers. An employer continues to be legally obligated to pay each laborer at or above the legally specified per-hour level, even if a new laborer has agreed to accept a lower amount of remuneration. Minimum-wage obligations are typically made unwaivable in this fashion because a minimum-wage scheme would be highly precarious in the absence of such unwaivability. If some prospective employees are willing to toil for lower wages, and if they exercise legal powers to waive the legally prescribed minimum of per-hour remuneration, the prospective employees who would not otherwise have agreed to work at the lower rates will come under great pressure to do so – insofar as they wish not to remain unemployed. Very rapidly in most credible circumstances, then, a minimum-wage scheme would become inefficacious if the legal obligations imposed by it on employers were waivable. Accordingly, to uphold the protective purpose of such a scheme, a system of governance that introduces it will typically make unwaivable the legal duties which it establishes. Any prospective employee therefore lacks one of the key legal powers that would enable him or her to exercise control over a minimum-wage duty. (Any prospective employee also lacks most of the other legal powers that would enable such control, but I am here concentrating only on the power of waiver at the pre-violation stage.) Yet, because individuals will each lack that key power to control the duty owed by an employer, the champions of the Will Theory have to conclude that any typical minimum-wage law does not confer claim-rights upon individuals to be paid at or above a certain per-hour level. If a lawyer who adheres to the Will Theory is asked by a client whether the client has a legal claim-right to receive a minimum per-hour level of remuneration from his or her new employer, the theoretical allegiances of the lawyer call for a negative answer even though a minimum-wage statute is operative in the jurisdiction where the question has been posed.

Fourth, what has aroused more outspoken condemnation than any other feature of the Will Theory is its exclusion of various types of beings from the category of potential holders of claim-rights. Because the Will Theorists insist that competence to make the sorts of choices required for controlling the duties of others is essential to the status of anyone as a potential holder of claim-rights, they are committed to affirming that only human adults of sound mind can ever hold any claim-rights. Among the beings excluded by the Will Theory from the category of potential holders of claim-rights are babies, infants, most children, insane people, people afflicted with dementia, permanently comatose people, fetuses, dead people, future generations of human beings, and all non-human animals. No such beings are capable of holding any claim-rights that will be acknowledged as such by the Will Theorists, because no such beings are capable of choosing non-fortuitously between exercising Hohfeldian powers and refraining from exercising those powers.

A diehard supporter of the Will Theory will be inclined to applaud the restrictions imposed by that theory on the class of potential holders of claim-rights. For example, Nigel Simmonds opines as follows with reference to the holding of claim-rights by infants (1998, 226 n.138):

> As regards moral rights, there is surely much merit in the claim that our moral concern for very small children is based on a concern for their welfare quite independently of their choices; as they grow older, some of our duties towards them come to be contingent upon their will. Is not this moral difference aptly reflected by the Will Theory of rights?

Still, regardless of how confident many of the Will Theorists have generally been in the correctness of their stance on this matter, the most frequent source of dissatisfaction with the Will Theory is the insistence by its proponents that infants and demented people and sundry others cannot hold any moral or legal claim-rights.

Fifth, although sundry claim-rights and other Hohfeldian entitlements possessed by people can be waived or transferred or forfeited, not all Hohfeldian entitlements are relinquishable in those ways – either as a matter of law in most jurisdictions or as a matter of the correct principles of morality. One's claim-right not to be subjected to lethal torture, for example, is insusceptible to being waived or forfeited. Similarly, one's claim-right against the lopping off of one's limbs by anybody else is insusceptible to being forfeited or waived (except in circumstances of medical exigency where the amputation of one's limbs is necessary for saving one's life). Likewise, one's claim-right and immunity against being sold permanently into slavery cannot ever be waived or forfeited. These claim-rights and certain other claim-rights are accompanied not by powers of waiver and forfeiture but instead by disabilities and their correlative immunities. So accompanied, the claim-rights are entrenchedly fortified against being extinguished or suspended during the life of a person who possesses them. Precisely because of the entrenchedness of those claim-rights, however, the Will Theorists are committed by their doctrine to denying that such entitlements are genuine claim-rights at all. As has been observed, the Will Theorists contend that the holder of any claim-right is vested with paired Hohfeldian powers of control at each of the three stages of a duty/claim-right relationship. For any claim-right like the ones mentioned here, the holder of the claim-right does not possess any power of waiver – or forfeiture or transfer – at the pre-violation stage of the claim-right's existence. Consequently, the Will Theorists have to conclude that each such apparent claim-right is not really a claim-right. (Of course, any holder of a claim-right not to be subjected to lethal torture will have ceased to exist at the post-violation and post-judgment stages of enforceability and will therefore lack any

Hohfeldian powers at those stages. Accordingly, as I have already maintained in regard to the broader claim-right against being murdered, any Will Theorists who concentrate on those subsequent stages of a duty's existence will insist that a claim-right against being subjected to lethal torture is not genuinely a claim-right. Here, however, I am concentrating on the pre-violation phase of a duty's existence. With a focus on that phase, the Will Theorists will reach the same negative conclusion about a claim-right against being subjected to lethal torture, but they will also reach such a conclusion with reference to the other unwaivable claim-rights that have been mentioned here and indeed with reference to any unwaivable claim-rights.)

Neil MacCormick forcefully derided the stance of the Will Theorists on these fundamental inalienable claim-rights (1977, 195–199). As MacCormick pointed out, such claim-rights inherently protect the vital interests of a party who holds them, whereas many alienable claim-rights inherently protect some considerably less important aspects of a party's situation such as the presence of paltry gewgaws in his or her residence. Yet the Will Theorists perceive those latter claim-rights as veritable claim-rights while insisting that the inalienable claim-rights which inherently protect vital interests are not properly classified as claim-rights at all. Now, although the Will Theorists are correct in thinking that one's legal and moral claim-rights against being deprived of one's gewgaws are genuine claim-rights, they go badly astray in presuming that certain entrenched fundamental duties which inherently protect the basic interests and autonomy of individuals are not correlated with any claim-rights held by those individuals. The fact that such claim-rights are insusceptible to being waived or forfeited is a hallmark of their centrality in any morally decent human interaction, yet that very feature of insusceptibility or entrenchedness removes those claim-rights from the category of claim-rights in the eyes of the Will Theorists. Some or all adherents of the Will Theory might be in favor of the legal unwaivability and unforfeitability of the legal duties that are correlated with those claim-rights – and some or all adherents of the Will Theory might recognize that the legal immunities which establish the unwaivability and unforfeitability are properly classifiable as legal rights – but they will outlandishly insist that the duties are not correlated with any claim-rights vested in the individuals whose basic interests are inherently protected by the duties.

### 2.4.2 A Powerful Objection That Does Not Beg the Question

Correct and forceful though the foregoing objections to the Will Theory are, their dialectical effectiveness is curtailed by the fact that each of them begs the question against the Will Theory. In the course of reaching the conclusion that the Will Theory is fallacious, each of the foregoing objections is premised expressly or enthymematically on the proposition that the Will Theory is fallacious. As a result, most of the Will Theorists tend to be unfazed by each of those criticisms. To be sure, as is evidenced by the fact that Hart partly retreated on the question whether infants are capable of holding legal claim-rights (Kramer 2024, 261–264), not all Will Theorists are wholly unattuned to the potency of the strictures that have been outlined so far. Nevertheless, the persuasiveness of those strictures in the mind of any Will Theorist is quite predictably lessened by the fact that each of them presupposes the unsoundness of the Will Theory.

I have therefore elsewhere devised a couple of critiques of the Will Theory that are not question-begging (Kramer 2024, 268–290). In the first of those critiques – the only one that can be summarized in this volume – I have endeavored to show that the Will Theory is nearly eliminativist in its implications. That is, I have shown that the Will Theorists through their analyses of right-holding have committed themselves to the proposition that there are very few instances of the holding of claim-rights anywhere. Of course, the Will Theorists have always insisted that there are far fewer instances of the holding of claim-rights than the advocates of the Interest Theory have supposed. When the Will Theorists discount the criticisms of their theory that have been marshaled hitherto, they are in effect contending that the people who voice those criticisms have greatly overestimated the numerousness of the circumstances wherein legal duties are correlated with legal claim-rights that are vested in the parties whose interests are inherently protected by the duties. Even so, the Will Theorists have certainly not been propounding a conception of right-holding that is deliberately eliminativist. They have not sought to come up with an analysis of the holding of claim-rights which begets the conclusion that there are hardly any instances of the holding of claim-rights. On the contrary, the Will Theorists such as Simmonds believe that their account of the holding of claim-rights is illuminatingly and distinctively applicable to the realm of private law in any jurisdiction (Simmonds 1998, 141–145). Whereas the Will Theorists dismiss the notion that legal claim-rights are conferred upon individuals by criminal-law prohibitions or by regulatory statutes such as minimum-wage laws, they affirm that the legal duties imposed by institutions of private law in any jurisdiction are correlated with legal claim-rights vested in the individuals whose interests are inherently protected by the duties. Admittedly, unlike an Interest Theorist, a Will Theorist does not maintain that the reason for classifying those individuals as holders of the specified legal claim-rights is that their interests are inherently protected by the correlative legal duties. Rather, a Will Theorist submits that the reason for so classifying those individuals is that the institutions of private law endow them with legal powers of control over the existence and enforcement of the correlative legal duties. As Simmonds declares: "[R]ights are primarily characteristic of private law: they exist within public law only in those special contexts (such as the conferment of welfare benefits) where public law is employed to secure particular benefits for individuals. The concept of a 'right', on this account, is strongly linked to the value of individual choice, and to the primacy of private law in protecting such choices" (1998, 141–142).

In my first main critique of the Will Theory that does not beg any questions, I have therefore demonstrated that the Will Theory's explication of the holding of claim-rights will generate the conclusion that the institutions of private law confer very few legal claim-rights (Kramer 2024, 268–284). By the reckoning of the Will Theorists, *malgré eux*, the vast majority of the legal duties imposed by those institutions are not correlated with legal claim-rights vested in individuals or organizations. By the reckoning of the Will Theorists, in other words, there are very few instances of the holding of claim-rights within the realm of private law. And since the Will Theorists contend that private law is the sphere in which instances of the holding of claim-rights distinctively occur, those theorists turn out to be inadvertently espousing the proposition that there are very few such instances anywhere. Their doctrine is nearly eliminativist in its implications. Moreover, that aspect of the Will Theory can be highlighted without any begging of the question.

In *Rights and Right-Holding*, my exposure of the nearly eliminativist character of the Will Theory is lengthy with many details and responses to potential rebuttals that cannot be included here.[6] Instead, only a bare sketch of my critique can be presented within the confines of this Cambridge Elements volume. Rather than proceeding explicitly or implicitly from the premise that the Will Theory is fallacious, my critique begins with two default rules. Any legal duty imposed by a system of governance will be within the scope of one or the other of these two background rules. (Although it is always true that one or the other of the two default rules is operative in relation to any given legal duty, it is not always true that one or the other of the two rules has been consciously adopted as such by legal officials or by anyone else beforehand. The operativeness of the default rule applicable to any particular duty might become apparent only after the duty has come into existence.) Of course, a system of governance need not rely solely on one type of default rule to the exclusion of the other. It

---

[6] See especially Kramer (2024, 279–284), where I mull over some versions of the Will Theory that are more modest than the conception of right-holding propounded by Hart (and by Hart's followers such as Hillel Steiner). I argue there that those moderate versions have abandoned the essence of the Will Theory in favor of the essence of the Interest Theory.

can employ one of the two default rules for some legal duties and the remaining default rule for other legal duties. For every legal duty D, however, there must be operative some default rule – perhaps not knowable beforehand – concerning what is to happen if no legal power to keep D in existence is exercised and no legal power to discontinue the existence of D is exercised. Notwithstanding that the two default rules can be modified to cover any of the three stages of a duty's existence (pre-violation, post-violation, post-judgment), our concern here is solely with the pre-violation stage. Accordingly, the two default rules are as follows:

**Default Rule 1:** If no power to keep a duty in existence has been exercised, the result shall be the permanent or temporary discontinuation of the duty.

**Default Rule 2:** If no power to cancel or suspend a duty has been exercised, the result shall be the continued existence of the duty.

As has already been noted, the pre-violation stage of a duty's existence is especially important because every duty is in that stage at some point and because most duties (by dint of being uncontravened) do not ever go beyond that stage. By concentrating on the pre-violation situation, we can discern why the Will Theory in the domain of private law is nearly eliminativist in its implications. Under the sway of Default Rule 2 as applied to some legal duty D, a party does not have a legal power to keep D in existence; a Hohfeldian legal power is an ability to change some legal positions, rather than an ability to keep all positions unchanged. An ability to keep positions completely unchanged is a Hohfeldian immunity or a set of Hohfeldian immunities, rather than a Hohfeldian power. Thus, when a duty in the realm of private law at the pre-violation stage is within the sway of Default Rule 2 (as is almost always the case), a legal power to terminate or suspend the duty is not coupled with any legal power to preserve the duty.

At the pre-violation juncture, where some private-law duty has not been contravened, the party whose interests are inherently protected by the duty – or else a representative of that party – will almost always be vested with a legal power to cancel or suspend the continued existence of the duty. However, that legal power of cancellation or suspension is very rarely accompanied by any converse legal power of retention. Usually no power of the latter sort is involved, because the persistence of a duty over time (through the fact that no power of waiver has been exercised) is not itself due to the exercise of a power of retention. A Hohfeldian legal power is an ability to *alter* some legal relationships, whereas the persistence of a legal duty usually involves the *retention* of all legal relationships as they are. Thus, instead of being due to the exercise of a legal power, the continuity of a private-law duty over time is attributable to an array of legal immunities. It normally consists in leaving things entirely as they are, rather than in changing things. In sum, because a power of retention if exercised would transform legal relationships, the notion of any such power at the pre-violation stage of the existence of a private-law duty is usually a phantasm – since the preservation of a duty at that stage usually consists in leaving legal relationships wholly unchanged. Consequently, at the pre-violation stage, the party whose interests are inherently protected by the existence of a private-law duty is endowed with a power of waiver over the duty but not normally with any power of retention.

What is so disquieting for the Will Theorists is that these observations about the pre-violation stage of any duty's existence are applicable to nearly every private-law duty. My observations have pointed to a difficulty that encompasses the vast majority of the duties in every system of private law. A proponent of the Will Theory maintains that the holder of a claim-right correlative to any private-law duty is vested with paired powers of waiver and retention (concerning that duty) at the pre-violation stage of the duty's existence. However, because it is very seldom true in any system of private law that somebody endowed at the pre-violation stage with a power of waiver over a duty D is endowed with a power of retention concerning D at that stage, the proponents of the Will Theory have committed themselves to the proposition that very few legal claim-rights are established by any system of private law. Without paired powers of waiver and retention in the hands of any single person at the pre-violation stage of a duty's existence, there is no claim-right recognizable as such by the Will Theory. A theory which treats the realm of private law as its special sphere of application has turned out to carry the nearly eliminativist conclusion that very few legal claim-rights are conferred by any institutions of private law.

Admittedly, the Will Theory's account of the holding of claim-rights is nearly eliminativist rather than thoroughly eliminativist, because some legal duties within the realm of private law are kept in existence through the exercising of legal powers rather than solely through legal immunities. For example, the owner of a private road in England typically has to perform certain actions periodically for the purpose of keeping in place the legal duties that require members of the public to refrain from using the road as a thoroughfare. Churchill College (Cambridge) as the owner of a private road has to obstruct it at least once a year in order to retain the status of the road as private. When the porters of Churchill College block off the road with traffic cones on Christmas Day each year, they are exercising some legal powers on behalf of the college to keep in existence the legal duties that are incumbent on members of the public. In so doing, the porters are altering the legal positions of the college by removing some quasi-liabilities – some quasi-liabilities of the college to lose certain legal entitlements – and by replacing them with a set of legal immunities.[7] *Pari passu*, the porters are altering the legal positions of members of the public by removing some quasi-liabilities (some quasi-liabilities of members of the public to gain certain legal entitlements) and by replacing them with legal disabilities. Such changes in the present legal relationships are necessary for keeping in existence the legal claim-rights and other legal entitlements that are possessed by Churchill College as the owner of a private road. Hence, the college is vested not only with legal powers to waive those claim-rights and other entitlements but also with legal powers to retain them.

Nonetheless, although there are some claim-rights in the realm of private law which are of that kind – where the holders of the claim-rights are endowed both with legal powers to terminate or suspend the correlative legal duties and with legal powers to keep those duties in existence – most claim-rights in the realm of private law are not of that kind. With regard to the large majority of the claim-rights that obtain in the realm of private law, their holders possess legal powers to terminate or suspend the correlative legal duties but not any legal powers to preserve those duties in existence. Instead, what secure the continued existence of the duties are various legal immunities. For example, my claim-right not to be defamed by anyone else or my claim-right not to be harmed by anybody else's negligence is scarcely kept in existence through my wiggling of my fingers or my dancing of a jig. Rather, each of those claim-rights remains in existence through the presence of sundry legal immunities that avert the extinguishing of each of those claim-rights (and through my not having performed any action that would constitute the waiving of either of those claim-rights). In that respect, each of those claim-rights is like nearly every one of my other claim-rights in the realm of private law.

Let us note afresh that my critique of the Will Theory as a nearly eliminativist account of the holding of claim-rights does not beg the question. That critique unfolds from my exposition of the two default rules, an exposition that does not presuppose the fallaciousness of the Will Theory in any way. I originally developed the gist of that exposition in quite a different context, without any reference to the Will Theory and its weaknesses and without my yet having realized that my sketch of the two default rules could be turned against the Will Theory. Indeed, that original presentation is in an article that bears the name of

---

[7]  In the domain of law, quasi-powers – which I discuss at length in Kramer (2024, 83–87) – are abilities to alter legal relationships where those abilities are possessed by natural entities and forces (such as thunderbolts and earthquakes and microorganisms) or by certain general laws such as statutes of limitations. A quasi-liability is of course a position of susceptibility to the transformative effects of the exertion of a quasi-power. Such a position of susceptibility can be occupied by anyone who is a potential occupant of any of the standard Hohfeldian legal positions.

Hillel Steiner – one of the foremost champions of the Will Theory – as a notional co-author.[8] My discussion there of the default rules does not proceed from any assumptions about the necessary and sufficient conditions for the holding of a claim-right. It instead simply proceeds from reflections on the conditions under which various legal duties are preserved or eliminated. Those reflections can then get parlayed into an attack on the Will Theory's analysis of the holding of a claim-right – as has been done here – but they do not themselves presuppose anything about the nature of claim-rights or about the nature of the holding of claim-rights. Furthermore, the conclusion directly drawn from those reflections is not even that the Will Theory is fallacious. Rather, the conclusion directly drawn from them is that the Will Theory is nearly eliminativist as an account of the holding of claim-rights. Of course, from the fact that the Will Theory is nearly eliminativist as such an account, I believe that one can soundly infer that the Will Theory is fallacious. Still, the proponents of the Will Theory could seek somehow to defend the proposition that their analysis of the holding of claim-rights is correct in being nearly eliminativist.

This point about my not having begged any questions is noteworthy, for the broadsides leveled by Interest Theorists and Will Theorists against each other are often perceived (and are quite often correctly perceived) as question-begging. Partly because the charges traded between the two camps in the Interest/Will debates have seemed question-begging to quite a few onlookers, the debates themselves have struck those onlookers as irresolvably deadlocked. Appeals for the discontinuing and transcending of the Interest/Will debates have proliferated, along with attempts to develop hybrid approaches. Accordingly, by presenting a far-reaching critique of the Will Theory that plainly does not beg any relevant questions, this discussion has gone some way not only toward resolving those debates but also toward establishing that they have been worthwhile.

## 2.5 A Capacious Version of the Interest Theory of Right-Holding

I lack space here to examine some possible rejoinders by the Will Theorists to my critique – rejoinders which I have parried in Kramer (2024, 279–284) – and I similarly lack space to elaborate my other main innovative objection to the Will Theory (Kramer 2024, 284–290). We need to move on to a capacious version of the Interest Theory of right-holding, which encapsulates the individually necessary and jointly sufficient conditions for the holding of any Hohfeldian entitlement that is properly classified as a right. A capacious version

---

[8] Kramer and Steiner (2007, 286–288). The ideas and prose in the 2007 article are mine, but Steiner played a key role in urging me to write it, and he read it carefully in advance of my submission of it for publication.

of the Interest Theory that comprehends all four categories of Hohfeldian entitlements must obviously be formulated differently from the way in which I have formulated the main version of the Interest Theory specifically with reference to claim-rights and their correlative duties.

One thing to be noted at the outset is that I am not aiming to present a version of the Interest Theory that would encompass every instance of each of the four broad Hohfeldian entitlements. Such an aim would be bootless, for the general categories of powers and immunities in Hohfeld's schema are evaluatively open-ended. Countless powers and immunities are typically beneficial on balance for the parties who hold them, and countless powers and immunities are typically detrimental on balance for the parties who hold them. Powers and immunities of the latter sort are not properly classified as "rights." Although the Interest Theory in its principal form (the form that has hitherto been expounded in this Elements volume) applies to every claim-right, multitudinous powers and immunities are beyond the scope of the capacious version of the Interest Theory that will be expounded now.

To arrive at the expansive version of the Interest Theory, we should ponder the sorts of entitlements in each Hohfeldian category that are aptly designated as "rights." As has just been remarked, many instances of the entitlements in the two higher-order categories of Hohfeld's schema are not aptly so designated. Let us contemplate, for example, a scenario of a malefactor who alters his own legal positions and the legal positions of constables or other law-enforcement officials through his perpetration of a crime. In that scenario the miscreant has exercised some legal powers through his perpetration of a crime, but in any ordinary circumstances those powers are not accurately characterizable as "rights." Quite ludicrous in any ordinary circumstances is the notion that the miscreant has exercised some legal rights by undertaking his criminality through which he has rendered himself legally liable to be arrested and placed on trial. Such a scenario, which illustrates the breadth of the Hohfeldian category of legal powers, can also alert us to the basis for differentiating between Hohfeldian entitlements that are appositely classifiable as "rights" and Hohfeldian entitlements that are not appositely classifiable in that manner. In other words, it can alert us to the criterion that should be encapsulated in a capacious version of the Interest Theory of right-holding:

> **Capacious Version of the Interest Theory:** A party $X$ holds a right if and only if (1) $X$ is endowed with a Hohfeldian claim-right or liberty or power or immunity of some type, and (2) being endowed with a Hohfeldian claim-right or liberty or power or immunity of that type is typically beneficial on balance for anyone like $X$.

Note that this formulation does not need to include a third clause which would affirm that $X$ belongs to the class of potential holders of Hohfeldian entitlements. After all, the first clause presupposes that $X$ does indeed belong to that class.

At a level of high generality, this wide-ranging version of the Interest Theory enables us to discern which Hohfeldian entitlements count as "rights" and which Hohfeldian entitlements do not so count. For instance, by recourse to it we can easily conclude that the legal powers of a wrongdoer to alter his own legal positions detrimentally through his transgression of a criminal-law prohibition are not legal rights. Precisely because the possession of those legal powers is typically disadvantageous on balance for somebody like the wrongdoer, his possession of them is not an instance of any holding of legal rights on his part. Although this verdict serves to ratify any credible pre-theoretical understanding of the scenario of the wrongdoer, the Capacious Version of the Interest Theory fortifies such an understanding by distilling what underlies it.

## 2.6 What Types of Beings Can Hold Claim-Rights?

In the main version of the Interest Theory of right-holding, which pertains specifically to the holding of claim-rights, the second enumerated clause provides that a necessary condition for the holding of any claim-right by $X$ is that $X$ belongs to the class of potential holders of claim-rights. In other words, no being can ever actually hold any legal claim-rights unless that being is capable of holding claim-rights.

Operative here is a distinction between the class of potential holders of claim-rights and the class of actual holders of claim-rights. Although every being in the latter class is also in the former class, the converse does not perforce obtain in the realm of law. For example, suppose that animals of a certain species are potential holders of claim-rights and that those animals are nonetheless not legally protected at all in some jurisdiction J. No typically beneficial aspects of the situations of such animals are inherently protected by any of the legal duties which the system of governance in J has established. Within J, then, animals of the species envisaged here are not actual holders of any legal claim-rights even though they are potential holders of such claim-rights. If some typically advantageous aspects of their situations were inherently protected by legal duties in J, then these animals would hold legal claim-rights correlative to the duties. However, because no such aspects of their situations are in fact inherently protected by any legal duties that have been established there, the status of these animals as potential holders of legal claim-rights is not matched in J by their status as actual holders of legal claim-rights. The fact that they would hold legal claim-rights within J if any typically beneficial aspects of their situations were inherently protected by duty-imposing laws there is due to their inclusion in the class of potential holders of claim-rights; the fact that they do not actually hold any legal claim-rights in J is due to the specifics of the duty-imposing laws there, which do not furnish any inherent protection for typically advantageous aspects of the situations of these animals.

To be sure, in the domain of *morality* there is not ever any similar incongruity between the extension of the class of potential claim-right-holders and the extension of the class of actual claim-right-holders. Everyone included in the former class is also included in the latter. Every being who can hold claim-rights at all is inherently protected, under the objectively correct principles of morality, against various forms of mistreatment. Even so, the distinction between the two classes is as important in the realm of morality as in the realm of law. My concern at this juncture is to suggest how the class of potential holders of claim-rights is to be demarcated – an endeavor that cuts across the distinction between morality and law, since every potential holder of moral claim-rights is also a potential holder of legal claim-rights and vice versa. Neither in regard to the purview of law nor in regard to the purview of morality is the present portion of this Elements volume concerned to chart the *actual* holding of claim-rights. Within the realm of law, the actual holding of claim-rights is an empirical and evaluative matter pertaining to the contents of the sundry duty-imposing laws in each jurisdiction. Within the realm of morality, the actual holding of claim-rights is a justificatory matter that pertains to the vast array of duties imposed by the objectively correct principles of morality. A project of pinning down the actual holding of moral claim-rights would involve a complete exposition of those principles – something beyond the scope of what can be done here. Still, although this Elements volume does not aspire to specify in any detail the moral claim-rights with which people are endowed, the second half of the volume will sketch some of the major justificatory approaches that have been pursued by philosophers (including me) in their efforts to specify what those moral claim-rights are.

One additional preliminary point of clarification is advisable here. As will be emphasized subsequently, the category of potential holders of claim-rights is not necessarily coextensive with the category of beings who are thought to be potential holders of claim-rights in this or that society. Misconceptions can lead people astray in either of two directions. Jurists and other citizens of some country might incorrectly think that certain beings in the class of potential holders of claim-rights are not within that class. Alternatively, or additionally, jurists and other citizens might err by thinking that certain beings outside that class are in fact within it. A misconception of the former type would obtain, for example, in a society where all non-human animals or some human beings are believed to be incapable of holding any claim-rights. A misconception of the latter type would obtain in a society where inanimate entities such as rivers or insentient organisms such as trees are believed to be capable of holding claim-rights. Misconceptions of each kind are not figments of my imagination. They have occurred in many actual societies, and in various forms they continue to occur. My brief ruminations here will seek to explain why such mistaken perceptions are indeed mistaken. At this stage, we should simply note that the contours of the class of potential claim-right-holders are not determined by what the people in any particular country take those contours to be. Determinative of the scope of that class are objective ethical and conceptual considerations, rather than the variable perceptions to which people cling. Whereas the patterns of actual right-holding are of course variable across societies and across historical periods, the breadth of the category of potential claim-right-holders – my present focus – is not similarly a jurisdiction-specific matter. We shall return to this point in due course.

### 2.6.1 Why Delimit the Class of Potential Holders of Claim-Rights?

Unlike the Interest Theory, the Will Theory of right-holding in itself delimits the class of beings who are recognizable by the theory as potential holders of claim-rights. Given the tenor of the Will Theory, with its insistence on competence as a precondition for the holding of any claim-rights, the class of potential holders of such entitlements is confined to human adults who are of sound mind. Only sane human adults possess the cognitive and deliberative faculties that are constitutive of the competence which the devotees of the Will Theory regard as essential for the holding of claim-rights. Only such adults are capable of making the moderately sophisticated choices that are involved in exercising powers of control over the existence and enforcement of duties. Consequently, as has been recounted already, the votaries of the Will Theory believe that all beings other than sane human adults are excluded from the category of potential holders of claim-rights. Babies and infants and embryos and fetuses and demented people and insane people and permanently comatose people and dead people and non-human animals and future generations of human beings are all perceived by the Will Theorists as falling outside that category. Hence, a book-length exposition of the Will Theory would not need any discussion like the present one (though it would of course need to attempt to defend the way in which the Will Theorists delimit the category of potential holders of claim-rights, since their severe narrowing of that category has elicited more animadversions over the past several decades than has any other feature of their theory). No discussion of this present kind would be required, because any elaboration of the Will Theory would already demarcate the class of potential holders of claim-rights. A restrictive delimitation of that class is internal to the main tenet of the Will Theory in combination with some elementary empirical observations about the cognitive and deliberative capacities of various types of beings.

By contrast, the Interest Theory in itself leaves open how broad or cabined the range of potential holders of claim-rights is. The Interest Theory is consistent with a highly circumscribed range such as that which is integral to the Will Theory, but it is also consistent with any much more expansive range. Interest Theorists usually maintain that the category of potential holders of claim-rights does extend far more broadly than the Will Theorists allow; I do not know of any Interest Theorist who has endorsed the Will Theory's insistence that only human adults of sound mind are capable of holding claim-rights. Still, the Interest Theory per se is consistent with any theses about the confinedness or embracingness of the class of potential holders of claim-rights.

Precisely because the Interest Theory itself can indeed be conjoined with any such theses, the current discussion is needed. My presentation of the Interest Theory will not be satisfactory unless the second enumerated clause of the theory has been explicated adequately. To grasp vividly the need for a disquisition on the scope of that clause, we should mull over some contrasts between certain types of legal mandates. Consider first a law that prohibits the perpetration of unprovoked violence by any human being against any other human being. Correlated with the legal duty borne by each person under such a law is a legal claim-right held by everyone else in the jurisdiction, a legal claim-right not to be subjected to unprovoked violence. After all, the existence of that legal duty inherently protects an aspect of the situation of each human being – an aspect that consists in not being subjected to such violence – which is typically beneficial on balance for anybody. What is more, although the inclusion of every human being in the class of potential holders of claim-rights will be confirmed and explained later, it can here safely be taken as given. Hence, the deontic upshot of the statute that prohibits the perpetration of unprovoked violence is the conferral of a legal claim-right upon every human being in the jurisdiction vis-à-vis everyone else there. Such a conclusion about the upshot of that statute is fully in accordance with the Interest Theory of right-holding and is likewise in accordance with most credible pre-theoretical understandings of the matter. (At least in application to mentally incapacitated human beings, the aforementioned conclusion goes beyond what the proponents of the Will Theory would acknowledge. Whether the Will Theorists would accept that each sane human adult Q holds a legal claim-right vis-à-vis everyone else under the statute is dependent on whether Q holds legal powers of control over the existence and enforcement of the legal duty that is incumbent on everyone else not to subject Q to unprovoked violence.)

Let us now contemplate an ordinance in some municipality that legally forbids people to walk upon the grass in the areas of a public park that have been marked with signs. Under the ordinance, each person in the jurisdiction bears a legal duty to refrain from walking on the grass in any of the designated areas. Correlated with that legal duty of each person is a legal claim-right to compliance, held by the system of governance that has enacted the ordinance. By deontically requiring each person to conform with a mandate which that system of governance has promulgated, the duty borne by each person inherently protects an aspect of the situation of the system that is typically advantageous for it on balance. Does any other party hold a legal claim-right correlative to the legal duty imposed by the ordinance on every member of the public? Such a duty inherently protects an aspect of the situation of the grass in the park – an aspect that consists in not being trampled upon – which is typically advantageous on balance for organisms like the grass. Indeed, the chief effect of the ordinance resides in its promotion of the flourishing of the grass. Should we therefore conclude that the grass holds a legal claim-right correlative to the legal duty imposed on each person by the ordinance? Should we conclude that each individual blade of grass holds such a claim-right?

Let us now envision a law that prohibits the defacement or culpable damaging of Old Master paintings. Under such a law, every person in the relevant jurisdiction bears a legal duty to refrain from defacing or otherwise culpably damaging any Old Master painting. A duty with that content inherently protects an aspect of the situation of each painting that is typically beneficial on balance for such an object. Each painting will be in a better condition if the legal duty of every person which pertains to it is fulfilled than if that duty is contravened. Should we thus conclude that the Old Master paintings are holders of legal claim-rights correlated with the duties borne by members of the public under the posited law? Instead of merely pertaining to those works of art, are the duties owed to them?

A final law to be mulled over at this juncture is a statute that proscribes the perpetration of vandalism. Such a statute imposes a duty on every person in the jurisdiction to forbear from culpably inflicting damage on buildings or other structures. A duty of that sort inherently protects an aspect of the situation of each building that is typically beneficial on balance for any such erection. Myriads of actions that would worsen the condition of any building affected by those actions are made legally wrong under the interdictory sway of the statute. Should we conclude that each edifice in the jurisdiction holds a legal claim-right correlative to the legal duty imposed on every person by the anti-vandalism law? Is that duty owed by every person to each edifice, as well as to the system of governance that has imposed the duty?

Of central importance here is that the Interest Theory does not in itself supply answers to any of the questions posed in the last few paragraphs. In each of the scenarios in those paragraphs, the first enumerated clause of the Interest Theory is satisfied in application to entities of a certain kind (grass, paintings, or buildings). Thus, the questions posed by the scenarios are in effect asking whether the second enumerated clause of the Interest Theory is also satisfied. As is apparent, my formulation of the Interest Theory does not without amplification enable us to judge whether the second clause of the theory is satisfied or not.

Very likely, most readers at a pre-theoretical level will concur with me in thinking that grass and paintings and buildings are not included in the class of potential holders of claim-rights. Most readers will probably likewise concur with me in thinking that human beings – at the very least, human adults of sound mind who are currently alive – are included in that class. Consequently, if my conjectures about the pre-theoretical inclinations of most readers are correct, those readers will share my sense that the law which forbids the perpetration of unprovoked violence against other people has conferred upon each person vis-à-vis everyone else a legal claim-right not to be subjected to such violence. And those readers will also share my sense that the laws which prohibit vandalism and walking on the grass and defacement of Old Master paintings have not conferred any legal claim-rights upon buildings or grass or paintings. Still, however widely endorsed those conclusions may be, they are not sufficient for the purposes of a philosophical account of right-holding. Until they are furnished with a theoretical basis, those conclusions do not lend themselves to generalization. Similarly, until they are furnished with such a basis, they cannot be adequately defended against challenges. Challenges are not unlikely, since very few conclusions in the philosophy of rights and right-holding are wholly uncontroversial. For example, although I am not aware of any philosophers who have endeavored to argue that paintings and buildings are among the potential holders of claim-rights, there have certainly been philosophers and jurists who have argued that insentient organisms such as grass and trees are among those potential holders. Just over half a century ago, for instance, Christopher Stone in a classic article contended that trees can and should hold legal rights (Stone 1972). Quite a few environmental ethicists have jousted with one another over the question whether certain inanimate natural entities such as rivers or stone formations can and should hold legal rights (Barkham 2021; Kramer 2017, 136; Kurki 2019, 127–131; Kurki 2022; Stockwell 2022). In sum, given the diversity of the positions that have been staked out by philosophers and jurists on these issues and on related issues, and given the need for extrapolating from one's stances on certain matters to appropriate stances on quite different matters, a pre-theoretical comprehension of the upshots of the several laws sketched here is patently not enough for coming to grips with the complexities of differentiating between the beings who are capable of holding claim-rights and the beings that are not so capable. We need to move beyond pre-theoretical convictions in order to gain a principled understanding – a richly theoretical understanding – of the category of potential holders of claim-rights.

### 2.6.2 Brief Observations on the Class of Potential Holders of Claim-Rights

I have elsewhere endeavored at length to supply the richly theoretical understanding to which I have here just referred (Kramer 2024, 292–388). In this Elements volume, I have to confine myself to sketching a few points. One important point is that the distinction between beings who are among the potential holders of claim-rights and beings that are not among those potential holders is different from the distinction between beings whose interests should receive ample legal protection and beings whose interests should not receive such ample legal protection.

Thus, for example, the following two propositions are perfectly consistent:

(1) Wherever legal norms impose duties on people not to abort any fetuses, those norms have thereby endowed the fetuses with legal claim-rights against being aborted.

(2) As a matter of substantive morality, first-trimester fetuses should not be legally protected against abortions in any jurisdiction (except insofar as abortion-inducing actions are malicious or reckless or negligent).

Proposition 1 does not prescribe the extent to which or the ways in which the interests of fetuses should be legally protected. It does not prescribe in favor of the establishing of certain legal duties, nor does it prescribe against the establishing of those duties. It does not say anything about the moral justification for bringing any legal duties into existence, and it does not say anything about the moral justification for keeping any legal duties out of existence. No such justificatory matters are addressed by proposition 1. Instead, it addresses the non-justificatory question whether fetuses are included in the class of potential holders of claim-rights or not. It presupposes that the answer to that question is affirmative, as it declares that fetuses hold legal claim-rights-not-to-be-aborted wherever people are under legal duties not to abort fetuses. Those legal duties inherently protect aspects of the situations of fetuses that are typically beneficial on balance for such beings; consequently, because fetuses are capable of holding legal claim-rights, the specified duties are correlated with legal claim-rights held by fetuses in any jurisdiction where the duties exist. Such is the thesis articulated by proposition 1, which does not take any stance on the moral justifiability or unjustifiability of the specified duties.

By contrast, proposition 2 comes to grips with one of the chief justificatory matters from which proposition 1 prescinds. It affirms that legal duties requiring people to abstain from aborting first-trimester fetuses are morally unjustified (except when malice or recklessness or negligence is involved). It concerns the degrees to which and the ways in which the vital interests of fetuses should be legally protected. With its focus on such justificatory questions, it leaves unaddressed the non-justificatory issue tackled by proposition 1. That is, it leaves unaddressed the question whether the legal duties requiring people to abstain from aborting first-trimester fetuses would be correlated with legal claim-rights held by the fetuses. More generally stated, it leaves unaddressed the question whether fetuses are included in the class of potential holders of claim-rights or not.

Divergent though proposition 1 and proposition 2 are in their respective orientations, they are straightforwardly consistent. Neither of them entails the other, but neither of them excludes the other. Somebody can quite coherently endorse both of them or only one of them or neither of them. I have here been addressing only the matter broached by proposition 1, and I will shortly endorse proposition 1. I have not here been musing upon the justificatory topic with which proposition 2 engages, even though I would endorse proposition 2 if its topic were under consideration here.

Similarly consistent are the following two propositions:

(3) When the law in any jurisdiction secures arboreal welfare by placing people under legal duties not to engage in activities that are injurious to trees, those duties are not correlated with any legal claim-rights held by trees.

(4) As a matter of substantive morality, trees should be legally safeguarded through the imposition of legal duties which obligate people not to undertake certain activities that would be injurious to trees.

Like proposition 1, proposition 3 does not address any justificatory questions. It does not take any stand on the extent to which or the ways in which the interests of trees should be legally shielded. It does not articulate any verdict on the moral justifiability or unjustifiability of the legal duties to which it refers. It instead takes a position on the non-justificatory question whether insentient organisms such as trees are among the potential holders of claim-rights. It presupposes that the answer to that question is negative – for it declares that, when legal duties inherently protect aspects of the situations of trees that are typically beneficial on balance for such organisms, the trees do not hold any legal claim-rights correlated with those duties.

This negative answer to the question about the status of trees as potential holders of claim-rights is entirely consistent with proposition 4. Instead of pronouncing upon that non-justificatory question about the extension of the class of potential claim-right-holders, proposition 4 pronounces upon a justificatory matter. It asserts that the imposition of extensive legal duties on people to protect the well-being of trees is morally justified in any jurisdiction. Its expression of solicitude for trees is unproblematically compatible with proposition 3, as can be inferred from the fact that a Will Theorist such as Nigel Simmonds is an avid environmentalist. Simmonds's insistence that only sane human adults can hold claim-rights is readily conjoinable with his further insistence that natural organisms such as trees should receive stringent legal protection that will promote their flourishing. Each of those stances adopted by Simmonds is an ethical doctrine, but the ethical issues on which he concentrates as a Will Theorist are quite distinct from the ethical issues on which he concentrates as a champion of environmentalist campaigns.

Keeping in view these distinctions between justificatory topics and non-justificatory topics that pertain to the holding of claim-rights, we can descry an additional dichotomy that is of cardinal importance for anyone who seeks to come to grips with the latter topics. That is, we need to differentiate between beings *for whom* various legal duties are imposed and beings merely *in regard to which* various legal duties are imposed. Beings of the former sort are the subjects, rather than merely the objects, of legal relationships. Beings of the former sort are included in the class of potential holders of claim-rights. When typically advantageous aspects of their situations are inherently protected by legal duties that have been established, such beings hold legal claim-rights correlative to those duties.

I have argued at length elsewhere that all living human beings and all future generations of people and many dead human beings are among the subjects of legal relationships (Kramer 2024, 317–388). They are beings for whom various legal duties are imposed on others, as they hold legal claim-rights that are correlated with those duties. I have further argued that most non-human animals are among the subjects of legal relationships. Those animals too are within the category of potential holders of claim-rights. Any animal comprised by that category holds legal claim-rights insofar as legal duties inherently protect aspects of its situation that are typically beneficial on balance for creatures like it. Alongside human beings, most non-human animals are creatures of ultimate value. Their possession of such value is what makes them subjects of legal relationships *for whom* – rather than solely *in regard to which* – those relationships are brought into existence.

Here we cannot delve into any of the details of the arguments which I have marshaled elsewhere in support of the conclusions just outlined. Instead, we can simply glance at the notion of ultimate value that has just been invoked, and we can then glance further at the basis for assessing whether beings are endowed with ultimate value. Ultimate value is possessed by beings if and only if (1) they are *êtres pour eux-mêmes* and (2) the furtherance of their interests is intrinsically valuable. Several points are in need of elucidation here.

First, I have used a variant of the Sartrean French phrase "*être pour soi*" rather than the English phrase "conscious beings" mainly in order to leave open a certain question which I have not needed to settle and have not sought to settle. Specifically, my recourse to the French phrase leaves open the question whether artificial-intelligence mechanisms might at some time in the future become so sophisticated and adroit in their capacities for reflection upon themselves – and for the adaptation of themselves accordingly – that they will then be properly included in the class of potential holders of claim-rights even if they are not conscious in the manner of human beings and other animals. At present, the best tack in response to the development of artificial-intelligence mechanisms is to leave open the question whether eventually some such mechanisms will fall within the class of potential holders of claim-rights.

Second, the phrase "*êtres pour eux-mêmes*" should obviously not be miscon-strued as an indication that a key to the possession of ultimate value and thus to inclusion in the class of potential holders of claim-rights is extravagant selfish-ness or solipsism. Like the Sartrean wording of which it is a variant, my phrase simply indicates that a key to the possession of ultimate value – and thus to inclusion in the class of potential holders of claim-rights – is a level of reflective attunedness that is characteristic of conscious engagement with oneself and with the world. Though human beings and most animals are selfish or self-absorbed to varying degrees, dispositions of those kinds are not at issue in my conception of ultimate value and in my efforts to demarcate the category of potential holders of claim-rights. At issue instead are much more general faculties of self-reflection and contemplation and adaptability and sophisticated alertness to one's environs.

Third, if we leave aside the matter of artificial-intelligence mechanisms, we can easily discern that inanimate beings and insentient organisms do not possess ultimate value. Trees and grass and plants and fungi are all excluded from my conception of ultimate value, as are countless inanimate entities such as paint-ings and symphonies and poems and rivers and canyons and hammers and nails and jigsaws and the property of freedom or generosity. Immensely valuable though many such entities are, they are not endowed with ultimate value and are therefore not potential holders of claim-rights. They are not *êtres pour eux-mêmes*. Legal duties can and should be established to protect many of those things, but the legal claim-rights correlated with any such duties are not held by those things themselves. Although the inanimate or insentient beings stand to benefit through the establishment of legal duties that inherently safeguard aspects of their situations which are typically advantageous on balance for beings like them, they are the objects to which the duties pertain rather than the subjects for whom the duties are introduced.

Of course, the exclusion of all insentient and inanimate phenomena from the class of potential holders of claim-rights is entailed by the first of the two components in my conception of ultimate value. That exclusion might thus seem arbitrarily stipulative. However, I have elsewhere sought at length to vindicate my conception of ultimate value by elaborating a rationale for delimiting the class of potential holders of claim-rights along the lines envisaged here (Kramer 2024, 292–388). Far from being arbitrarily stipulative, the two clauses in my formulation of ultimate value are grounded on the deepest ethical principles that underlie the inclusion of beings in the category of potential holders of claim-rights.

A rationale of the kind just mentioned is clearly needed, for the exclusion of certain insentient and inanimate beings from the property of ultimate value and from the class of potential holders of claim-rights is not wholly uncontroversial. As has already been remarked, quite a number of environmental ethicists have contended that insentient organisms such as trees and plants can hold claim-rights, and some legislatures as well as environmental ethicists have presumed that certain inanimate entities such as rivers and coral reefs and canyons can hold claim-rights. Laws that expressly purport to confer legal claim-rights upon such entities are currently existent in some jurisdictions.

As is obvious, a full-scale justification for my conception of ultimate value – and therefore for my account of the class of potential claim-right-holders – cannot be presented within the tight confines of this Elements volume. Only the barest outline can be furnished here. Any satisfactory justification must begin by recognizing that sane human adults are the paradigmatic potential holders of claim-rights. They are central to the class of potential holders of claim-rights, both because their membership in that class is uncontroversial and because their moral obligations to recognize the membership of certain other beings are central to determining the class's contours.

Whence do those moral obligations derive? They are grounded in the paramount moral responsibility of every sane human adult. While the paramount moral responsibility of every system of governance is to bring about the political and social and economic conditions under which everyone in a society can be warranted in harboring a strong sense of self-respect, the paramount moral responsibility of every sane human adult is to contribute to the realization of those conditions. When we ask which beings the paradigmatic members in the class of potential holders of claim-rights are morally obligated to recognize as also within that class, we are asking whether the inclusion or exclusion of certain beings would be consistent with the satisfaction of the paramount moral responsibility incumbent on each of those paradigmatic members. There are two chief dimensions to such an enquiry: the import of the inclusion or exclusion of certain beings for those beings themselves, and the import of the inclusion or exclusion of certain beings for the paradigmatic potential holders of claim-rights.

Pursuing the lines of inquiry just mentioned, I have elsewhere arrived at the following conclusions (Kramer 2024, 333–388). No inanimate entities or insentient organisms are among the potential holders of claim-rights; most non-human animals are among those potential holders; collectivities of human beings and all individual human beings who are alive at any given time are among the potential holders of claim-rights; many dead people and all future generations of people are also among those potential holders. In *Rights and Right-Holding* I provide detailed argumentation in favor of each of these conclusions, but unfortunately we cannot explore any of the details here. Instead, my present remarks on the class of potential holders of claim-rights will close with a caveat. Somebody who agrees with me about the basis for membership in the class of potential holders of claim-rights will not necessarily agree with every one of my concrete conclusions about the beings who are included in that class or excluded therefrom. There is ample leeway for Interest Theorists to disagree among themselves over the precise extension of the category of potential claim-right-holders. There is no canonical specification of that extension which every Interest Theorist must endorse in order to remain an Interest Theorist. Although I have endeavored elsewhere to stake out the boundaries of the aforementioned category through lengthy reasoning, my cardinal objective herein has been to delineate the proper basis for the inclusion of beings within that category and for the exclusion of beings from it. Any Interest Theorist who disagrees with me over the specific locations of the boundaries can nonetheless concur with me about the basis for identifying them.

## 3 Moral Justifications for Assignments of Legal Rights

Heretofore in this Elements volume, we have investigated what claim-rights and other Hohfeldian entitlements are, and we have plumbed the conditions that are necessary and sufficient for the holding of claim-rights. Henceforward, we will examine some of the main approaches that have been developed by political philosophers for morally justifying certain distributions of legal entitlements. In other words, we shall here be mulling over some of the justificatory questions from which I have prescinded in the first half of this volume. Such questions cover the extent to which and the ways in which the interests of various parties should be legally protected through the bestowal of claim-rights or immunities, and the extent to which and the ways in which the interests of various parties should be legally furthered through the bestowal of liberties or powers. Such questions also cover the fundamental justifications for the conferral of these legal entitlements.

Within the constraints of this Elements volume, I cannot undertake any survey of prominent theories of justice that have been propounded in bygone centuries. The focus here will have to lie on the past several decades, and even in regard to that confined period of time my engagement with different approaches to justice will have to be highly selective. Philosophers have come up with multitudinous theories of justice from the 1970s onward, yet we can investigate only a handful of those theories – none of them in any depth.[9] By far the most salient account of justice throughout the period under discussion is the one offered by John Rawls in his 1971 book *A Theory of Justice* and in some of his subsequent writings such as his 1993 tome *Political Liberalism* and his 2001 volume *Justice as Fairness*. My reflections on Rawls will therefore be more detailed than my reflections on any of the other philosophers who will be considered here.

## 3.1 Contractualism and the Rawlsian Principles of Justice

In philosophers' meditations on distributive justice during the past several decades, a common methodological step resides in distinguishing between concepts and conceptions. Whereas a concept is thinly abstract, a conception fleshes out the elements of the concept by developing them in specific directions. Associated with the concept of distributive justice, then, are multiple conceptions advanced from diverse perspectives. Wariness is advisable, however, for the concept/conception dichotomy is misleadingly tidy. My invocation of that dichotomy might convey the impression that only two levels of theoretical exposition are involved. In fact, we can best understand and situate the principal contemporary accounts of justice among several different layers of theoretical development.

---

[9] For some of the works with which I would engage if the constraints of this volume were less confining, see Anderson (1999); Cohen (2008); Frankfurt (2015); Freeman (2007); Gauthier (1986); Miller (1999); Mills (1997); Nozick (1974); Nussbaum (2006); Okin (1989); Scanlon (1998); Sen (2009); Young (1990). I have engaged with most of those works, critically but fruitfully, in some of my other writings.

Fittingly enough, the book that has been the fountainhead of disputation about justice among contemporary philosophers – Rawls's *A Theory of Justice* – is also, within political philosophy, the *locus classicus* for the distinction between concepts and conceptions. To be sure, that distinction did not originate with Rawls. He himself attributed it to Hart (Rawls 1971, 5 n1), and it existed in various guises long before Hart. Still, the following comments by Rawls have been particularly influential in shaping the methodological orientation of philosophers who have written in recent decades about matters of distributive justice:

> Men [and women] disagree about which principles should define the basic terms of their association. Yet we may still say, despite this disagreement, that they each have a conception of justice. That is, they understand the need for, and they are prepared to affirm, a characteristic set of principles for assigning basic rights and duties and for determining what they take to be the proper distribution of the benefits and burdens of social cooperation. Thus it seems natural to think of the concept of justice as distinct from the various conceptions of justice and as being specified by the role which these different sets of principles, these different conceptions, have in common. Those who hold different conceptions of justice can, then, still agree that institutions are just when no arbitrary distinctions are made between persons in the assigning of basic rights and duties and when the rules determine a proper balance between competing claims to the advantages of social life. Men [and women] can agree to this description of just institutions since the notions of an arbitrary distinction and of a proper balance, which are included in the concept of justice, are left open for each to interpret according to the principles of justice that he accepts. These principles single out which similarities and differences among persons are relevant in determining rights and duties and they specify which division of advantages is appropriate. Clearly this distinction between the concept and the various conceptions of justice settles no important questions. It simply helps us to identify the role of the principles of social justice. (1971, 5–6, footnote omitted)

As this passage suggests, the concept of distributive justice is thin by Rawls's reckoning. It can best be understood as denoting the appropriate assignments of basic Hohfeldian legal entitlements and the appropriate apportionments of the benefits and burdens of social interaction among the members of any community. Such a formulation leaves open what counts as "appropriate," what counts as "basic," what count as "benefits" and "burdens" and "social interaction," and what counts as a "community." Hence, it covers illiberal conceptions of justice as well as all liberal conceptions.

However, more than one level intervenes between that thin concept and Rawls's conception of justice as his two lexically ordered principles that are applicable to the major legal-governmental institutions of any society. Rawls's conception is one of many liberal conceptions, each of which differs from any illiberal conceptions. For Rawls, the hallmark of the heterogeneous liberal conceptions of justice is their convergence on certain tenets about the nature of persons and the nature of the societies wherein persons dwell and interact. More specifically, all the liberal conceptions of justice concur in deeming persons to be free and equal and in affirming that any morally legitimate society is a fair arrangement for social cooperation. They further share the premise that individuals who are not subject to coercive or manipulative thought-control will reasonably diverge from one another in the course of arriving at a multiplicity of views about what is valuable in life.

The notion of fairness invoked at this point is not yet a distinctively Rawlsian notion; it is a much roomier idea that can accommodate many theories of justice which are strongly opposed to Rawls's theory. For example, many varieties of utilitarianism will be classifiable as liberal conceptions in that they are compatible with the tenets just broached. Similarly, Robert Nozick's libertarianism and quite a few other varieties of libertarianism will qualify as liberal theories. By including in his theory a Lockean proviso as an encumbrance on the legitimacy of private appropriation, Nozick aligned himself – albeit somewhat tenuously – with thinkers who take legitimate societies to consist in fair arrangements for social cooperation. A host of other free-market thinkers, such as Friedrich Hayek and Milton Friedman, are likewise classifiable as liberals by Rawls's reckoning.

Notwithstanding that many libertarian and utilitarian accounts of justice could be recognized by Rawls as broadly liberal, he did not regard all such doctrines as fully reasonable. He of course did not believe that his own conception of justice was the lone fully reasonable conception, but he did maintain that liberal theories are not fully reasonable unless they partake of certain features of his own theory.[10] Specifically they have to accept that every citizen is to be endowed with basic legal rights and liberties, and that those basic rights and liberties are to enjoy special priority over other considerations of political morality. Fully reasonable liberal theories likewise accept that every citizen should possess adequate general means for exercising the basic rights and liberties. At this level of theoretical ramification, then, nearly all varieties of utilitarianism and some further varieties of libertarianism are excluded as not fully reasonable.

In reaching the level of theoretical ramification just mentioned, Rawls proceeded with a constructivist methodology. That is, he posited a situation of

---

[10] On Rawls's account, two or more theories can be fully reasonable — in that they each accept all the tenets recounted here — even though one of the theories is more reasonable than the other(s). Rawls explicitly took reasonableness to be a scalar property: "[A] conception of justice is reasonable in proportion to the strength of the arguments that can be given for adopting it in the original position" (1971, 352).

ideally rational agents who all endorse the fundamental tenets of liberalism recounted above, and he educed the conclusions at which they would arrive under ideal conditions of deliberation – the "Original Position" – from which all morally arbitrary or improper factors have been excluded by a Veil of Ignorance. However, the constructivist methodology is just one way of supplying a framework for processes of moral reasoning (processes of moral reasoning by philosophers about justice) that are subject to certain normative constraints. Those normative constraints are reflected in the idealization of the parties' deliberations in the Original Position, but they can perfectly well instead be incorporated more directly into the reasoning of political philosophers. What is crucial for Rawls's project is the compliance with those constraints, rather than the specific method for complying with them.

Having moved from the level of liberal theories of justice to the level of fully reasonable liberal theories of justice, Rawls then expounded his own conception of justice as the two complex principles that have been so extensively discussed ever since the publication of *A Theory of Justice*. That is, he maintained that a proper account of justice comprises a first principle which requires that each person be assigned the greatest array of basic civil and political entitlements that will be compatible with the assigning of a similar array to everyone else; and an initial component of a second principle, which requires that positions of power and influence be open to every person on equal terms; and a latter component of the second principle, which requires that inequalities in entitlements to wealth and income be permitted only insofar as those inequalities are beneficial for the people who are least well-off. Whereas the first principle is thoroughly egalitarian with regard to outcomes, each component of the second principle potentially countenances some disparities among persons with regard to outcomes. Rawls's conception of justice is in rivalry with other contemporary conceptions that also qualify as fully reasonable liberal accounts of justice: prioritarianism, sufficientarianism, motley versions of egalitarianism, some varieties of libertarianism, and so forth. Unfolding through the different levels that have been recounted here, his elucidation of the concept of justice acquired enough definiteness to place it in competition with these other theories. (Of course, the levels or stages in the elaboration of Rawls's conception of justice are not as tidily demarcated in his writings as I might seem to be suggesting. His unpacking of the concept of justice proceeded through some of those levels or stages simultaneously. Nonetheless, they can and should be distinguished here analytically.)

I have not yet mentioned Rawls's most famous contribution to the methodology of philosophy: his notion of reflective equilibrium. Within the structure of conceptual analysis expounded above, reflective equilibrium is most notably sought in the transition from liberal theories of justice to fully reasonable liberal theories of justice. Rawls prodded his readers to contemplate their own firmest convictions about justice. Although those convictions can pertain to highly abstract matters as well as to more concrete matters, Rawls especially had in mind one's convictions about specific ways of treating other people. His examples in his opening discussion of reflective equilibrium indicate as much:

> There are questions which we feel sure must be answered in a certain way. For example, we are confident that religious intolerance and racial discrimination are unjust. We think that we have examined these things with care and have reached what we believe is an impartial judgment not likely to be distorted by an excessive attention to our own interests. These convictions are provisional fixed points which we presume any conception of justice must fit. (1971, 19–20)

With those provisional fixed points in view, Rawls's readers are then to examine his specification of the conditions that constitute the Original Position. Those conditions generate certain principles of justice, of course. What Rawls's readers need to ask themselves, on the way to attaining reflective equilibrium, is whether the principles of justice derivable from the Original Position are congruent with their considered convictions about justice. If a reader notes any discrepancies between those principles and her convictions, she then needs to determine how harmony between them can best be effected. She might decide that she needs to modify some of her considered convictions in order to bring them into line with principles of justice which she finds compelling, or she might instead decide that Rawls's principles are themselves in need of modification. If she does reach the latter conclusion, she will also have to specify the appropriate alterations in the conditions that make up the Original Position. As a reader seeks to reconcile the principles of justice with her own considered convictions, she might well undertake adjustments in both directions through several iterations of the process. As Rawls declared (1971, 20):

> We can either modify the account of the [Original Position] or we can revise our existing judgments, for even the judgments we take provisionally as fixed points are liable to revision. By going back and forth, sometimes altering the conditions of the contractual circumstances, at others withdrawing our judgments and conforming them to principle, I assume that eventually we shall find a description of the [Original Position] that both expresses reasonable conditions and yields principles which match our considered judgments duly pruned and adjusted. This state of affairs I refer to as reflective equilibrium.

Some of the controversial features of Rawls's Original Position, such as the ascription of maximin reasoning to the agents therein, are best understood as products of the attainment of reflective equilibrium. They are features which served to reconcile Rawls's principles of justice – the principles of justice that are to emerge from the Original Position – with his considered convictions.

In his later writings, Rawls distinguished explicitly between narrow and wide varieties of reflective equilibrium.[11] If we seek narrow reflective equilibrium, we are aiming simply to ensure that our considered convictions and our principles of justice fit together coherently. If we go further by striving for wide reflective equilibrium, we not only aim to achieve congruity between our convictions and our principles; in addition, we subject the convictions and principles to challenges by assessing them in the light of alternative perspectives. In other words, a theory of justice developed in wide reflective equilibrium is a doctrine whose tenets and implications have been tested against the pronouncements of the major rival theories of justice. When such a theory has been fashioned and refashioned in a process of attaining wide reflective equilibrium, its substantive soundness as well as its internal consistency has been put to the proof.

Though a quest for reflective equilibrium is not the sole element of Rawls's understanding of the way in which the concept of justice should be analyzed, it is the central element. Rawls's highlighting of it reveals that, in his view, the endeavor of conceptual analysis – that is, the elucidation of the boundaries and implications of the concept of justice – is in part a collaborative enterprise. To achieve wide reflective equilibrium in one's conception of justice, one must engage not only in ruminations on one's own ideas but also in dialogues with some alternative outlooks.

In short, the progress of Rawls's ruminations was as follows. Rawls began with a highly abstract concept of justice, and he then differentiated the liberal conceptions from the illiberal conceptions by maintaining that every one of the former conceptions converges both on the proposition that persons are free and equal and on the proposition that a society should be a fair arrangement for social cooperation. Additionally, the liberal conceptions all allow that individuals through their faculties of ratiocination and deliberation are apt to cleave reasonably to numerous different sets of priorities in their respective vocations and avocations. Rawls then proceeded to distinguish the fully reasonable liberal conceptions of justice from the liberal conceptions that are not fully reasonable, as he contended that each of the former conceptions affirms that every person

---

[11] The distinction between the wide and the narrow is first drawn explicitly in those terms in § 1 of Rawls (1974). However, the distinction itself (without the "wide"/"narrow" terminology) is present in Rawls (1971, 49–50).

should be endowed with basic civil and political liberties and claim-rights and powers and immunities. Fully reasonable conceptions of justice likewise accept that every person should possess sufficient resources for exercising those basic legal entitlements. Rawls employed his constructivist methodology – his thought-experiment of the Original Position – to arrive at his distinction between liberal conceptions that are fully reasonable and liberal conceptions that are not fully reasonable. Having drawn that distinction, he employed his constructivist methodology further to propound his two complex principles of justice. Throughout this progression in his layers of thought, Rawls was endeavoring to achieve and sustain a condition of wide reflective equilibrium. He did so as he sought to specify the extent to which and the ways in which the interests of persons should be protected through the conferment of legal claim-rights or immunities, and the extent to which and the ways in which the interests of persons should be furthered through the conferment of legal liberties or powers.

## 3.2 Ronald Dworkin and Constructive Interpretation

Although Ronald Dworkin invoked the distinction between a concept and its conceptions in some parts of his work, he disagreed with Rawls by trying to cast doubt on the availability of any formulable concept of justice. As he wrote (1986, 74–75):

> Political philosophers can . . . try to capture the plateau from which arguments about justice largely proceed, and try to describe this in some abstract proposition taken to define the "concept" of justice for their community, so that arguments over justice can be understood as arguments about the best conception of that concept. Our own philosophers of justice rarely attempt this, for it is difficult to find a statement of the concept at once sufficiently abstract to be uncontroversial among us and sufficiently concrete to be useful. Our controversies about justice are too rich, and too many different kinds of theories are now in the field. . . .. Perhaps no useful statement of the concept of justice is available. If so, this casts no doubt on the sense of disputes about justice, but testifies only to the imagination of people trying to be just.

Dworkin maintained that debates over justice are meaningful and coherent not because they are oriented toward some unifying formulation of a concept, but instead because the participants in those debates share a pre-theoretical understanding of the range of matters covered by the concept of justice – and because the participants likewise concur on an array of paradigmatic specimens of justice or injustice.

In the final book that he published during his lifetime, *Justice for Hedgehogs*, Dworkin continued to develop the account of interpretive concepts which he had first presented at length in the 1980s. As he declared: "We share these [interpretive] concepts [such as the concept of justice] not because we agree in their application once all other pertinent facts are agreed upon, but rather by manifesting an understanding that their correct application is fixed by the best interpretation of the practices in which they figure" (2011, 158). Dworkin thought that each of the practices involving interpretive concepts is held together not by the sharing of formulable criteria but by widespread agreement on paradigmatic cases. Philosophers who dispute with one another about the concept of justice are offering rival sets of principles – rival conceptions of the concept – under which the paradigmatic cases of justice can be subsumed and thereby vindicated. Those principles extend beyond the paradigmatic cases to other matters on which there is no widespread agreement. Because the disputants adhere to divergent sets of principles, they wrangle intractably over the non-paradigmatic cases even though their argumentation is anchored in their shared recognition of the paradigms as such.

Now, although Dworkin's approach to pinning down the extension of the concept of justice is plainly different from Rawls's approach, the two are not perforce incompatible. Dworkin, however, took Rawls to task for seeking to specify a concept of justice that sets forth criteria or decisive tests for the identification of items within the concept's extension. Everyone who shares the concept of justice is in agreement on the applications of those criteria or tests. Such is the view which Dworkin puzzlingly attributed to Rawls (Dworkin 2011, 166–167, footnote omitted, quoting Rawls 1971, 5):

> In [*A Theory of Justice*] John Rawls says that people who disagree about justice nevertheless "agree that institutions are just when no arbitrary distinctions are made between persons in the assigning of basic rights and duties and when the rules determine a proper balance between competing claims to the advantages of social life." It is far from plain, however, that people do agree on criteria even at that very abstract level. It is a popular view in some parts of the world, for instance, that political institutions are unjust when they fail to respect God by providing authority and preference to his priests. That opinion objects not when arbitrary distinctions are made but when necessary ones are not made, and the complaint contains no claim about the proper distribution of advantages created by social life.

In his criticism of Rawls, Dworkin returned to his assertion that the concept of justice does not lend itself to any helpful encapsulation (2011, 167):

> It is unclear that we can find any form of words, however abstract, that describes a consensus among those we take to share the concept of justice. But even if we could, that consensus would not describe a decision procedure for identifying justice or injustice. On the contrary, it would simply point to

further apparent disagreements, whose nature as genuine disagreements would then have to be explained. If we accepted Rawls's suggestion, for instance, we would have to identify criteria that people who disagree about justice all accept for determining which distinctions are "arbitrary" and what is a "proper" balance of advantages. There are no such criteria.

Though Rawls's very early work is vulnerable to Dworkin's chiding, his later work does not warrant any such reproaches. My overview of the structure of Rawls's theorizing – a structure within which Rawls explicated the concept of justice by searching for wide reflective equilibrium in his jousting with rival theories, especially with utilitarianism – does not rely at all on the notion of decision procedures whose outcomes or applications are recognized by every competent participant in discussions of justice. Rawls did not conflate determinacy and demonstrability in the manner condemned by Dworkin. To be sure, each of the layers in Rawls's reflections is marked by necessary and sufficient conditions. However, as has been indicated, those conditions at each level pertain to the inclusion of theories at that level. They are relatively concrete moral principles or values on which certain philosophers converge through moral reasoning after having already converged on more abstract points. Philosophers who instead arrive at other concrete moral principles or values have not misapplied some decision procedure that was immanent in the more abstract points of convergence.[12] Rather, they have engaged in alternative paths of moral reasoning. They have construed differently the values and principles on which they are in concurrence with other theorists at the more abstract level(s).

In other words, the pathways of conceptual explication in Rawls's work are broadly similar to those pursued by Dworkin. In neither case does the elucidation of the concept of justice proceed through criteria that are putatively applied alike by all competent participants in debates over justice. As is conceded in the last of the quotations from Dworkin above, the rejection of criterialism (in Dworkin's sense) is separable from the question whether the concept of distributive justice lends itself to being pithily formulated. Dworkin and Rawls parted ways over that latter question, but neither of them was thereby committed to the implausible model of conceptual explication which Dworkin imputed to Rawls.

---

[12] A defender of Dworkin might here point out that, in the structure of Rawls's theorizing, there is a transition from liberal accounts of justice to fully reasonable liberal accounts of justice. However, as has been remarked, that transition leaves ample room for fully reasonable theories of justice in competition with Rawls's own theory. Moreover, as has also been remarked, reasonableness is a scalar property; hence, the fact that certain theories fall short of being fully reasonable does not entail that they are straightforwardly unreasonable and therefore incompetent.

As for the matter of coming up with an encapsulation of the concept of distributive justice, Dworkin abandoned the quest rather precipitately. Consider, for example, the penultimate quotation above. There Dworkin objected to Rawls's meditations on the concept of justice by contending that, although Rawls's wording discountenances arbitrary differences among people in the distribution of basic rights and duties, it does not address any circumstances where a system of governance has failed to register some vital differences among people in the system's undertaking of such a distribution. Rawls could have responded very easily, by amplifying his wording to cover such circumstances explicitly. Given the ready availability of such a response, Dworkin did not come up with any demurrals that tellingly exposed some inadequacies in Rawls's concept-distilling efforts.

Moreover, when Dworkin specified a few of the paradigms which he took to be the unifying field of the concept of justice, he left himself vulnerable to some caviling doubts reminiscent of those which he raised against Rawls's delineation of that concept. He maintained that one of the paradigms is the unjustness of a situation in which a system of governance takes steps "to convict and punish someone known to be innocent of any crime" (2011, 161). If the innocence of a convicted person P is known only to legal-governmental officials – and is very unlikely ever to be known by anyone else – then there are many possible circumstances in relation to which a hard-core proponent of utilitarianism will be prepared to accept that the conviction of P for this or that crime is not unjust. Furthermore, even if P's innocence is known widely to members of the general public, there can be situations in which those members of the public will regard the conviction of P for a specified crime as just. For example, by the end of the trial in *To Kill a Mockingbird*, everyone in the courtroom knows that Tom Robinson has not perpetrated the crime of which he has been accused. Nonetheless, the jurors convict him, and they undoubtedly perceive their heinous verdict as just. In their eyes, the verdict rightfully underscores the status of a black man who has been accused by a white woman. Dworkin committed himself to saying that the jurors do not have any grasp of the general concept of justice, whereas Rawls could more plausibly aver that their grasp of that general concept is combined with their hideously illiberal understanding of what counts as an arbitrary distinction.

## 3.3 Value-Independence versus Value-Neutrality

Before we examine the approaches of a few more philosophers who have sought to articulate the chief bases for distributions of claim-rights and other Hohfeldian entitlements among the members of any community, we should take cognizance of an important distinction between value-independence and value-neutrality. If a project of theorizing is *value-independent* in the sense specified here, it is not grounded on any ethical values. That is, the justifications for its theses – justifications relied upon expressly or implicitly by someone who advances those theses – do not draw upon ethical values. Some values do of course inform and undergird any such project, but they are theoretical-explanatory or logical-mathematical or aesthetic rather than ethical.

*Value-neutrality*, in the sense specified here, is different. If certain theses are value-neutral, then we can gauge the fulfillment or non-fulfillment of those theses in any number of settings without having to undertake any ethical judgments. In other words, the presence or absence of the states of affairs recounted by those theses can be ascertained without any ethical assessments.

The distinction between value-independence and value-neutrality can perhaps best be illustrated with an example from a closely related area of political philosophy. Ian Carter in his theory of political and social freedom has addressed questions concerning whether individuals are free or unfree to adopt various modes of conduct, and he has likewise addressed questions concerning how free each person is overall (Carter 1999). Under Carter's theory, the answers to those questions can in principle be discovered – through formidably complex investigations – without any recourse to ethical judgments. We can answer those questions by ascertaining what people are able to do or unable to do, and by carrying out complicated aggregations of the magnitudes of their abilities and inabilities. Hence, by Carter's lights, overall freedom and particular freedoms and unfreedoms are value-neutral properties. However, his justifications for specifying the nature of freedom as he does are ethical through and through. Carter maintains that the value-neutral property which he singles out as overall freedom is of great moral significance in a number of respects that he carefully delineates. He contends that that property is a desideratum with reference to which we can make good sense of the theories of justice that prescribe how freedom should be distributed. Similarly, when Carter specifies the nature of particular freedoms and unfreedoms, he is doing so with an eye toward the ways in which they contribute to individuals' levels of overall freedom. In his view, then, overall freedom and particular freedoms and unfreedoms are all value-dependent phenomena even though they are all value-neutral phenomena. Their value-neutrality, indeed, is crucially related to their value-dependence – because, according to Carter, it is their value-neutrality that renders them promotive of the ethical values which he invokes as the justifications for the tenets of his theory.

In connection with justice as well, value-independence and value-neutrality are disseverable. Nearly all philosophers who seek to expound the concept of justice recognize that the task of conceptual explication is value-dependent. They recognize that the pertinent justifications for expounding the concept of justice in some direction(s) rather than in other directions are ethical. Yet, while every theory of justice is value-dependent, there can be theories of justice that are at least partly value-neutral. Suppose for example that a theory ascribes injustice to every distributive arrangement in which the annual income of any person surpasses some specified percentage of the gross national output produced by the country in which the person resides. If the measuring of a country's gross national output does not itself have to draw on ethical judgments, and if the measuring of each person's income likewise does not have to draw on any ethical judgments, then the threshold of injustice here posited is value-neutral. Without engaging in further ethical judgments, we can ascertain whether that threshold is exceeded in any given situation. Thus, although such an account of injustice is not value-independent, it is value-neutral. That is, although any credible justification for espousing such an account of injustice will be grounded in ethical values, the congruity or incongruity between the account's requirement and the distributive arrangements in this or that society can be gauged without recourse to ethical beliefs.

For clarification, we should here note a type of neutrality that is very different from the value-neutrality which I have just been recounting. As is evident in my earlier discussion of Rawls, an explication of the concept of justice typically progresses from a level of very high abstraction through levels of greater and greater concreteness. A position taken at a very high level of abstraction is logically consistent with most of the positions that can be taken at any of the more concrete levels of conceptual explication. In that respect, stances on the most abstract matters in one's cogitations about justice are neutral vis-à-vis myriad stances on any of the more concrete matters in those cogitations. Thus, for example, a philosopher who agrees with Rawls in his understanding of the general concept of justice can quite coherently dissent from Rawls's views when addressing some more concrete issues such as the soundness of the difference principle or the design of the Original Position or the tenability of a constructivist approach to theorizing. The connections between Rawls's abstract conceptual distillation and his principles of justice are substantive moral links rather than logical entailments. As a matter of logical consistency, his abstract conceptual distillation is neutral between his own principles of justice and a medley of rival principles.

Of course, the neutrality of a highly abstract formulation of the nature of justice – that is, its neutrality in relation to the more concrete understandings of justice – is not comprehensive. A concept that encapsulates the nature of justice (however abstractly) will have ruled out some possible conceptions of justice at more concrete levels. Still, although no encapsulation of the basic concept of justice is *comprehensively* neutral in relation to the more concrete doctrines of justice that might be propounded, any such encapsulation is neutral among a multifarious congeries of those doctrines. Of central importance here is that this neutrality of the abstract vis-à-vis the concrete is markedly different from value-neutrality. For example, whereas Rawls's abstract concept of justice is logically consistent with a host of concrete conceptions – and is therefore neutral among a host of such conceptions, in the sense specified by this paragraph and the preceding paragraph – it is not value-neutral. To the question whether the state of affairs required by that concept is currently an actuality, any germane answer must involve ethical judgments.

## 3.4 Hillel Steiner and Putative Methodological Austerity

Most contemporary political philosophers realize that the challenge of explicating the concept of justice is a morally laden endeavor rather than an austerely analytical or formal endeavor; the value-dependence of theories that expound the concept of justice has been recognized by most such philosophers, including both Rawls and Dworkin. Very few theorists aspire to explicate the notion of justice without relying on basic ethical tenets. However, there are a few mavericks. Most prominent among them throughout the past several decades has been Hillel Steiner.

Over the course of his career, Steiner has sought to establish normatively rich conclusions on the basis of exiguously formal premises. In that respect, his ambitions place him in a broadly Kantian tradition of theorists who attempt to endow moral conclusions with the prestige of logic (though of course not all philosophers who have been influenced by Kant are in sympathy with that methodological orientation). Steiner purports to present a detailed theory of justice through reasoning that is austerely focused on considerations of logical consistency. He believes that his theory will prevail if it avoids the incoherence that supposedly besets alternative conceptions of justice.

In the opening pages of his 1994 book *An Essay on Rights*, Steiner introduces the chief method which he will employ to answer questions of justice. Adverting to what he designates as a "compossibility test," he explains that method as follows:

> A set of rights being a possible set is, I take it, itself a necessary condition of the plausibility of whatever principle of justice generates that set. Any justice principle that delivers a set of rights yielding contradictory judgements about the permissibility of a particular action either is unrealizable or (what comes to the same thing) must be modified to be realizable. (Steiner 1994, 2–3)

Steiner declares that his compossibility test "does exemplary service in filtering out many candidate conceptions of justice," and he states that "[o]ur aspiration, obviously, is to pass through the eye of this needle with at least one theory of justice still intact" (Steiner 1994, 3).

Yet, far from being a stringent filter that singles out one theory of justice (or a very small number of theories of justice), Steiner's compossibility test is decidedly undemanding. It is satisfied by virtually every theory of justice that has ever been embraced by any reputable philosopher. Hardly any such theory generates the conclusion that some act-type or act-token is both morally permissible and morally impermissible.

Steiner adheres to a contrary view largely because of his belief that every morally obligatory course of conduct is morally permissible. He persistently asserts that "a duty to do an action implies a liberty to do it" (Steiner 1994, 86), and he likewise repeatedly insists that "obligatory actions form a [proper] subset of permissible actions" (Steiner 1998, 268 n55). He believes that any theory of justice is incoherent if it leaves room for situations in which people are morally forbidden to engage in morally obligatory courses of conduct. He broaches and applies his compossibility test on the basis of that belief. Hoping thus to rely exclusively on the compossibility test and a few other formal considerations for the vindication of his theory of justice, Steiner contends that a philosophical account of justice – and of connected phenomena such as liberty and moral rights – can and should be value-independent (as well as value-neutral). Such an account will explicate the concept of justice without having to draw upon moral and political considerations, or so Steiner thinks.

Elsewhere (Kramer 2009a; 2014, 2–19; 2024, 28–34), I have subjected Steiner's methodological stance to lengthy critiques and have thereby endeavored to show that any satisfactory analysis of the concept of justice must draw centrally upon considerations of political morality. Any such analysis is value-dependent. Someone who professes to be able to explicate the concept of justice on the basis of purely formal constraints is chasing after a chimera. In particular, Steiner systematically conflates "P is morally obligated not to φ" with "P is not morally obligated to φ," as he presumes that the former proposition contradicts "P is morally obligated to φ." When his confusion on that point is dispelled, and when we recognize the possibility and quite frequent actuality of moral conflicts – each of which involves a situation in which someone is under a moral duty to φ and is simultaneously under a moral duty not to φ – we are able to see that theories of justice can allow for the existence of conflicting moral duties while remaining logically impeccable. A situation in which I bear simultaneously a moral duty to φ and a moral duty not to φ is very different from an incoherent situation in which I owe Joe a moral duty to φ and in which I simultaneously am morally at liberty vis-à-vis Joe not to φ. Whereas the conflicting moral duties can perfectly well coexist even though they cannot ever be jointly fulfilled, the combination of a moral duty to φ and a moral liberty not to φ (held vis-à-vis the same party) cannot ever genuinely exist. Unlike conflicting moral duties, contradictory moral positions cannot be co-occurrent. By mistakenly presuming that conflicts between moral duties are contradictions or that they entail contradictions, Steiner concomitantly errs by presuming that theories of justice which allow for the possibility of conflicts between duties are transgressive of his compossibility test. On the contrary, such theories are perfectly coherent; his test does not sift out any of them. Of course, any account of justice that envisions the *pervasiveness* of conflicting duties (as opposed to their *occasional* presence) is problematic. However, the dubiousness of such an account resides not in logic but in substantive morality. As a substantive moral matter, principles of justice should not lead to the conclusion that people will very frequently be unable to avoid the perpetration of wrongdoing. If Steiner wishes to assail a theory of justice that does carry such a conclusion, he will have to contest it on moral grounds. His hope of dealing with the issue on logical grounds is illusory.

## 3.5 Joseph Raz and Tom Campbell on Methodological Engagedness

In his 1986 book *The Morality of Freedom*, Joseph Raz pondered whether the concepts of political freedom and justice lend themselves to being analyzed without recourse to substantive ethical considerations. In a subsection of his opening chapter entitled "The Inadequacy of Linguistic Analysis," Raz articulated his methodological stance robustly (1986, 15–16):

> [M]uch that has been written in articles and books purporting to define and elucidate or analyse the concept of freedom will be helpful to anyone interested in the issues to be explored here. Philosophers and political theorists are sometimes better than their word. Much that is presented as conceptual analysis is really much more and includes advocacy of principles of political freedom. Moral and political philosophy has for long embraced the literary device (not always clearly recognized as such) of presenting substantive arguments in the guise of conceptual explorations. One may even say that the whole purpose of [*The Morality of Freedom*] is to defend a concept of political freedom. It is only important to remember that that concept is a product of a theory or a doctrine consisting of moral principles for the guidance and evaluation of political actions and institutions. One can derive a concept from a theory but not the other way around.

This understanding of the role of conceptual analysis informed Raz's outlook in all the subsequent portions of his book. For example, when Raz discussed coercion, he wrote that "[w]hichever view one takes, it is not to be justified on linguistic or conceptual grounds but by the soundness of the moral theory of which it is a part." His conception of coercion "is not to be justified as a piece of ordinary language analysis but on the grounds that while in accord with the core meaning of coercion it fruitfully ties it to sound moral principles" (1986, 150, 151). As these quoted passages indicate, Raz did not deny that conceptual analysis focused on formal and linguistic considerations should play a role in the elaboration of a theory of justice. His point was simply that those considerations are markedly insufficient in themselves for the vindication of any such theory.

Tom Campbell, in the opening chapter of his well-known book on justice (2001, 9–13), similarly grasped that any adequate analysis of the concept of justice is value-dependent. Campbell did not distinguish between value-independence and value-neutrality – either in those terms or in any other terms – and some of his comments can be construed as referring to either of those properties. However, that distinction is less important in the present context than is his recognition that an analysis of the concept of justice has to go beyond formal and linguistic concerns. His emphasis on the value-dependence of conceptual analysis became especially palpable when he expressed some wariness of the distinction between concepts and conceptions.

Specifically, Campbell queried any understanding of the concept/conception distinction which assumes that "analyses of the concept of justice tell us what justice is all about in a detached and philosophical manner, while analyses of the differing conceptions of justice state what justice is in concrete terms and so enter the disputed arena of contentious and ideological political debate" (2001, 10). Like Raz, Campbell accepted that conceptual analysis focused on linguistic and formal considerations does have a place in any theorizing about justice, but – again like Raz – he contended that any such approach is insufficient on its own. As he declared (2001, 11):

> Further, the concept/conceptions distinction can be misleading if based on the assumption that there is a clear line of demarcation between a morally neutral, if highly general, concept of justice on the one hand and specific conceptions which embody substantive moral interpretations of the general concept on the other hand. This strategy does not allow for the possibility that the concept of justice itself represents a distinguishable moral point of view which puts limitations on what can reasonably count as a conception of justice.

Having shown alertness to the value-dependence (and also the value-non-neutrality) of theses that adumbrate the concept of justice, Campbell salutarily admonished his readers against packing too much substantive content into the abstract concept: "On the other hand, there is a danger of arriving at a restrictive analysis of the concept of justice which excludes rival political or philosophical views on an arbitrary basis." He dilated upon his concern:

> [T]he linguistic usages to which we appeal in order to establish a very specific concept of justice may be tendentious or dated, reflecting the experience and bias of the philosopher and their community rather than the alleged neutrality of ordinary and typical discourse. Analyses of the concept of justice which dictate its specific meaning may often be no more than devices for putting one set of values beyond the scope of critical evaluation. (2001, 12)

As Campbell's remarks suggest, the value-dependence of any endeavor to analyze the concept of justice is thicker and thicker as the analysis proceeds from the abstraction of the general concept to the textured concreteness of a conception. Even at the level at which the abstract concept is picked out, the identification of it has to rest on some very general moral values. As that abstract concept is then developed into a conception, the value-dependence of the whole enterprise becomes all the more manifest and more intricate. Though formal and linguistic concerns are operative as well, moral principles (at varying levels of abstraction and concreteness) are the indispensable matrix within which any theory of justice unfolds.

## 3.6 Lessons to Be Learned

Let us mull over three main lessons to be learned from this compendium of some of the ideas propounded by a few of the prominent philosophers who have grappled with questions about the justificatory foundations for any satisfactory distribution of claim-rights and other Hohfeldian entitlements.

### 3.6.1 Methodological Engagedness

One main lesson is quite apparent. Steiner goes badly astray when he supposes that his compossibility test can disqualify competing theories of justice as incoherent, for his supposition to that effect is grounded on his conflation of deontic conflicts and logical contradictions. Conflicts between duties (whether moral or legal) may often be regrettable ethically, but a predicament in which somebody bears a duty to φ and simultaneously bears a duty not to φ is logically unimpeachable. Predicaments of that kind are entirely possible and are sometimes actual. As Steiner errs egregiously on that point, he also errs more broadly in his aspiration to resolve far-reaching questions of political morality on analytical or logical grounds. Raz and Campbell, along with countless other political philosophers over the centuries, were correct in insisting that such questions have to be addressed through recourse to principles of political morality. Any sound alternative to the theories of justice summarized heretofore will have to be aligned with Raz and Campbell on this central matter of methodology and will therefore have to be positioned against Steiner.

### 3.6.2 Fundamental Premises

Another lesson to be learned from my expositions of a handful of contemporary theories about justice is that every such theory must take some moral principle or some set of moral principles to be foundational for any just distribution of legal claim-rights and other legal entitlements. We have seen as much already in my summarizing of Rawls's reflections on justice. Though the specific formulations advanced by Rawls during the course of his career were not completely static between *A Theory of Justice* and his later books *Political Liberalism* and *Justice as Fairness*, his fundamental premises remained constant. Throughout those works, he invoked the free and equal status of persons as a cornerstone of his theorizing. As he wrote in *Political Liberalism*:

> [C]itizens [are] free and equal persons. The basic idea is that in virtue of their two moral powers (a capacity for a sense of justice and for a conception of the good) and the powers of reason (of judgment, thought, and inference connected with these powers), persons are free. Their having these powers to the requisite minimum degree to be fully cooperating members of society makes persons equal. (1993, 19)

Another cornerstone of Rawls's theorizing was his conception of a well-ordered society as "a fair system of cooperation over time, from one generation to the next" (1993, 15). Rawls expanded on this thesis: "Cooperation involves the idea of fair terms of cooperation: these are terms that each participant may reasonably accept, provided that everyone else likewise accepts them. Fair terms of cooperation specify an idea of reciprocity: all who are engaged in cooperation and who do their part as the rules and procedure require, are to benefit in an appropriate way" (1993, 16). To the premise affirming that persons are free and equal and the premise affirming that any veritable society is a fair system of cooperation, Rawls added another foundational premise about the inevitable emergence of a plurality of ethical outlooks – including sundry reasonable ethical outlooks – among the members of any free society. As he observed: "The political culture of a democratic society is always marked by a diversity of opposing and irreconcilable religious, philosophical, and moral doctrines. Some of these are perfectly reasonable, and this diversity among reasonable doctrines political liberalism sees as the inevitable long-run result of the powers of human reason at work within the background of enduring free institutions" (1993, 3–4). In any society where extreme manipulation and oppression are not wielded, certain features of human beings and of the complicated ethical issues which they have to address are such as to ensure that human beings will disagree intractably over those issues even after careful rumination thereon. These convergence-thwarting features are what Rawls designated as the "burdens of judgment" (1993, 54–58). A premise affirming the operativeness of the burdens of judgment is the third foundation of Rawls's theorizing.[13]

Although far more could be said about the cornerstones of Rawls's account of justice, my current discussion does not require more than the foregoing sketch. Let us now consider the foundation of Dworkin's political philosophy. Even more clearly than Rawls, Dworkin was steadfast throughout his career in his understanding of the basis on which all his conclusions about matters of justice and matters of public policy rested. In his first book, *Taking Rights Seriously*, he included two important presentations of that basis. His initial comments on it occurred when he was delving into the fundaments of Rawls's account of the Original Position and the distributive principles that ensue therefrom. Dworkin contended that the deepest benchmark of equality which underpins Rawls's whole account of justice is as follows:

> [I]ndividuals have a right to equal concern and respect in the design and administration of the political institutions that govern them …. [P]olitical arrangements that do not display equal concern and respect are those that are established and administered by powerful men and women who, whether they recognize it or not, have more concern and respect for members of a particular class, or people with particular talents or ideals, than they have for others … .[Rawls's Original Position] is well designed to enforce the abstract right to equal concern and respect, which must be understood to be the fundamental concept of Rawls's deep theory … .This is one right, therefore, that does not emerge from the [social] contract, but is assumed, as the fundamental right must be, in its design. (1978, 180–181)

Dworkin concluded that Rawls's theory of justice "rests on the assumption of a natural right of all men and women to equality of concern and respect, a right they possess not by virtue of birth or characteristic of merit or excellence but simply as human beings with the capacity to make plans and give justice" (1978, 182).

In a later chapter of *Taking Rights Seriously*, Dworkin returned to the moral principle which was the foundation of his own political philosophy and which he had identified as the foundation of Rawls's political philosophy. He wrote as follows (1978, 272–273):

---

[13] For an exposition of Rawls's cogitations on the burdens of judgment, see Kramer (2017, 8–12).

Government must treat those whom it governs with concern, that is, as human beings who are capable of suffering and frustration, and with respect, that is, as human beings who are forming and acting on intelligent conceptions of how their lives should be lived. Government must not only treat people with concern and respect, but with equal concern and respect. It must not distribute goods or opportunities unequally on the ground that some citizens are entitled to more because they are worthy of more concern. It must not constrain liberty on the ground that one citizen's conception of the good life ... is nobler or superior to another's. These postulates, taken together, state what might be called the liberal conception of equality.

More than two decades later, Dworkin published his foremost book on the topic of equality. The title of that book, *Sovereign Virtue*, bespeaks the centrality of the principle of equal concern and respect in his political philosophy. He expounded that principle as a pair of precepts: "Two principles of ethical individualism seem to me fundamental . . ., and together they shape and support the account of equality in this book" (2000, 5). He elaborated (2000, 5):

The first is the principle of equal importance: it is important, from an object-ive point of view, that human lives be successful rather than wasted, and this is equally important, from that objective point of view, for each human life. The second is the principle of special responsibility: though we must all recognize the equal objective importance of the success of a human life, one person has a special and final responsibility for that success – the person whose life it is.

Dworkin proceeded to outline the upshot of each precept for any system of governance (2000, 6):

The first principle requires government to adopt laws and policies that insure that its citizens' fates are, so far as government can achieve this, insensitive to who they otherwise are – their economic backgrounds, gender, race, or particular set of skills and handicaps. The second principle demands that government work, again so far as it can achieve this, to make their fates sensitive to the choices they have made.

In his final book published during his lifetime, *Justice for Hedgehogs*, Dworkin again unfurled his cardinal principle of equal concern and respect as a pair of precepts. Near the outset of that tome, he declared (2011, 2):

No government is legitimate unless it subscribes to two reigning principles. First, it must show equal concern for the fate of every person over whom it claims dominion. Second, it must respect fully the responsibility and right of each person to decide for himself how to make something valuable of his life. These guiding principles place boundaries around acceptable theories of distributive justice – theories that stipulate the resources and opportunities a government should make available to people it governs . . . . [E]very distribution must be justified by showing how what government has done respects these two fundamental principles of equal concern for fate and full respect for responsibility.

Similar pronouncements recur throughout the closing portions of the book, as Dworkin foreshadowed in his introductory chapter:

> The question of distributive justice [addressed squarely in the concluding chapters] therefore calls for a solution to simultaneous equations. We must try to find a solution that respects both the reigning principles of equal concern and personal responsibility, and we must try to do this in a way that compromises neither principle but rather finds attractive conceptions of each that fully satisfy both. (2011, 3)

As Dworkin repeatedly reaffirmed when he turned to matters of justice in his closing chapters: "Coercive government is legitimate only when it attempts to show equal concern for the fates of all those it governs and full respect for their personal responsibility for their own lives" (2011, 352).

### 3.6.3 Against Constructivism

A third major lesson to be learned from my synopses of some of the most influential recent approaches to the justificatory foundations of rights is that the constructivist dimension of Rawls's theorizing is to be eschewed. As has been recounted, Rawls (especially in *A Theory of Justice* but also in his later tomes) proceeded by positing a situation of ideally rational agents whose deliberations fix upon principles of distributive justice that are morally incumbent on every political community. By specifying punctiliously the idealized conditions of the agents' deliberations and of the agents themselves, Rawls ensured that their conclusions would tally with his considered convictions about specific ways of treating people and about specific societal arrangements.

In *Justice for Hedgehogs*, Dworkin summarized astutely the purport of Rawls's constructivism: "Rawls … described his famous book, *A Theory of Justice*, as an exercise in 'Kantian' constructivism. On this view, moral judgments are constructed, not discovered: they issue from an intellectual device adopted to confront practical, not theoretical problems" (Dworkin 2011, 63). As Dworkin observed, Rawls interpreted Kant's first formulation of the Categorical Imperative in line with Rawls's own constructivist methodology: "Rawls gave the example of Kant's Categorical Imperative: Kant said that we must construct our moral judgments by asking what moral principles we could will as maxims to be followed not just by us but by everyone" (Dworkin 2011, 63). Taking account of Rawls's assertions on the matter, Dworkin submitted that Rawls through his constructivism was endeavoring to prescind from questions about the objective truth of the principles of justice which the parties in the Original Position embrace: "So we might understand constructivism, at least as Rawls understood it, not as itself providing a skeptical argument but rather as showing that moral truth need play no part in defending an attractive and detailed theory of political justice. Constructivism challenges [a role for objective truth] not directly but by trying to shove it aside" (Dworkin 2011, 65).

Dworkin accepted that a device such as the Original Position can be heuristically or expositorily valuable (2011, 64). It can solidify the confidence of a philosopher in the objective truth of some moral principles by enabling the philosopher to confirm that the principles in question are derivable from an attractive version of the Original Position. Similarly, it can facilitate one's efforts to ascertain some objectively correct moral principle(s) in the first place. Though the Original Position is not the source of the objective correctness, one's contemplation of the deliberations of the parties in the Original Position can help to elicit one's attention to morally pregnant features of situations which one might otherwise have overlooked. Still, while Dworkin readily allowed that a thought-experiment like the Original Position can be salutary in these ways, he firmly and rightly assailed Rawls's ambition to set aside questions about the objective truth of the principles that emerge from the Original Position. Dworkin convincingly argued that "Rawls's constructivist project, at least as he sometimes conceived it, is impossible" (2011, 66).

A couple of years before Dworkin marshaled his lines of reasoning against Rawls in *Justice for Hedgehogs*, I published some different lines of reasoning that make broadly the same points against Rawls and his followers. In my *Moral Realism as a Moral Doctrine* (2009b, 67–69), I have shown that a contractualist apparatus like that of the Rawlsian Original Position is always redundant because its idealization of the parties within the apparatus has to incorporate the contents of all the correct principles of morality. Unless the parties to the ideal contractualist deliberations are perfectly informed of all correct moral principles and all the implications of those principles, their deliberations will be prone to generate erroneous determinations. It is not enough that the ideal parties are perfectly rational and perfectly well motivated and perfectly acquainted with all relevant empirical facts. Parties flawless in all those ways might still adhere to incorrect moral principles. Through moral ignorance, the contractualist parties who are perfect in rationality and motivation and empirical knowledge might nonetheless endorse some incorrect moral precepts or decline to endorse some correct moral precepts. If the outcomes of their deliberations are to be infallible touchstones of rightness and wrongness and other moral properties, the parties will have to grasp exhaustively the contents and implications of all the correct principles of morality. Yet, given that the contractualist model is not guaranteed to yield correct results unless the parties are indeed approvingly attuned to all the aforementioned contents and implications, the whole model is superfluous. The correctness of the results of the parties' deliberations is guaranteed only insofar as the parties cleave unswervingly to the correct principles of morality when they arrive at those results. In other words, the justificatory basis for any apt conclusions about principles of justice resides entirely in the correct principles of morality; the device of the deliberating parties is completely dispensable. Any true conclusions pertinently reachable by a contractualist philosopher through that device are so reachable only because they follow from the correct principles of morality.[14]

A slightly different way of putting this point is that the deliberations of the ideal contractualist parties will lack any justificatory force unless the idealized conditions of the deliberations and the idealized traits of the parties are endowed with justificatory force. However, on pain of vicious circularity, the fact that those conditions and traits are endowed with justificatory force cannot itself be effected through the deliberations of the contractualist parties. It cannot itself be one of the authoritative outcomes which it has to antecede as the source of their authoritativeness. Instead of *ensuing* from the interaction of idealized parties, then, the correct standards of morality are *prior* to any such interaction as the provenance of all the justificatory force which that interaction possesses.

In short, contrary to what the proponents of some contractualist theories have presumed, the correct principles of morality are strongly mind-independent. Far from being derivative of the consenting responses of ideal agents under ideal conditions, those principles determine what the relevant idealization of the agents and the relevant idealization of the conditions are. Only inasmuch as those idealizations ensure that the contractualist parties will abide unfailingly by the correct principles of morality, do the contractualist deliberations generate authoritative results. Precisely because the contractualist model is thoroughly

---

[14] Rawlsians are likely to respond by accusing me of begging the question against them. However, when I insist on the determinativeness of moral principles that are prior to the deliberations of contractualist parties, I am doing directly what Rawls did obliquely through his search for reflective equilibrium. He embarked on that search for the purpose of specifying suitably the idealized conditions that are constitutive of the Original Position. As I have already indicated, his adjusting of those conditions to fit with his considered convictions about various modes of conduct was of major importance in shaping the Original Position. By undertaking the adjustments, Rawls ensured that the parties in his thought-experiment would be unfailingly oriented toward the moral principles that implicitly underlay the adjustments – moral principles which he of course believed to be correct. Rawls thus aptly recognized that his idealization of the parties and their deliberations had to incorporate the correct principles of morality; but his recognition of that point was far too oblique. My critique of contractualism underscores that point directly and robustly. In so doing, it reveals that the whole contractualist apparatus is redundant.

reliant on those principles for its own authoritativeness, however, the model is redundant as a wellspring of general requirements of justice. The correct principles of morality are themselves the sole necessary and sufficient wellspring of such general requirements.

Just as the arguments in my *Moral Realism as a Moral Doctrine* against contractualism anticipated the arguments developed by Dworkin a couple of years later in his *Justice for Hedgehogs*, so too I have anticipated him in allowing that a contractualist scenario of deliberations among ideal parties can be heuristically or expositorily illuminating (Kramer 2009b, 67–68). As I have written:

> [I]f the contractarian model is dissociated from the claim that the consenting responses of ideally rational agents would be *determinative* of the contents of moral principles and the extensions of moral predicates, that model might still be a valuable device for *identifying* those contents and extensions. Perhaps it sets forth a method of moral reasoning that will stand moral philosophers and other people in good stead. (2009b, 67–68, emphases in original)

Still, although contractualism might be heuristically or expositorily valuable in this fashion, it is of no value as an account of the basis for the contents and implications of the correct principles of morality. As I have remarked: "[W]hat will be challenged [in my critique of contractualism] is the notion that the consent of ideal contractarian agents would antecede and determine the moral order of the world" (2009b, 68). To the extent that Rawls assumed the contrary, he erred.

## 3.7 An Alternative Approach

Keeping in mind the lessons that are to be learned from my survey of some previous theories of the justificatory foundations for distributing legal claim-rights and other legal entitlements, we should now consider an alternative to those theories – an alternative which I have been devising and refining for the past decade-and-a-half. Unlike Steiner, but like each of the other political philosophers with whom I have engaged here, I readily recognize that the project of unearthing the aforementioned foundations has to be executed through ethical argumentation that draws upon principles of political morality. Considerations of logical consistency are vital, of course, but in themselves they are radically insufficient to underpin an account of how legal claim-rights and other legal entitlements should be distributed. Additionally essential are the substantive moral considerations that serve to differentiate sound from unsound principles of distribution.

Like Dworkin, but unlike Rawls, I eschew any constructivist methodology in my reasoning about matters of justice or indeed about any other ethical matters.

I do not appeal to any device like the Original Position, and I emphatically deny that the correctness of moral principles is somehow dependent on the fact that they would be recognized as correct by someone (such as the parties in the Original Position). Still, although my approach to these matters is unremittingly anti-constructivist, it resembles Rawls's approach as well as Dworkin's in that it postulates a fundamental moral principle on which it centers all its conclusions about the extent to which and the ways in which the interests of various parties should be legally protected through the conferral of legal claim-rights and other legal entitlements. We have encountered that fundamental principle already, in my meditations on the class of potential holders of claim-rights. I have there maintained that the paradigmatic members of that class – namely, human adults of sound mind – are morally obligated to recognize that various other beings are also members. What underlies those moral obligations of recognition incumbent on the paradigmatic members is the paramount moral duty borne by each of them. Whereas the paramount moral responsibility of every system of governance is to bring about the political and social and economic conditions under which everyone in a society can be warranted in harboring a strong sense of self-respect, the paramount moral responsibility of every sane human adult lies in seeking to contribute to the realization of those conditions. Such a responsibility ramifies far beyond the conclusions which sane human adults are morally obligated to reach about the membership of other beings in the class of potential holders of claim-rights.

In several of my previous books, I have explored how the paramount moral duty of every system of governance carries far-reaching implications for the ways in which legal claim-rights and other legal entitlements should be distributed. On matters of legal governance ranging from capital punishment to prohibitions on torture and from public subsidies for the arts to freedom of expression, that paramount moral duty requires any system of governance to undertake certain actions and to abide by certain constraints (Kramer 2011; 2014; 2017; 2021). As a deontological moral obligation that is binding always and everywhere, the paramount moral responsibility incumbent on every system of governance gives rise to a myriad of further deontological moral obligations that are likewise absolute in their bindingness.[15] I have charted some of those further obligations in the books to which I have just referred, and

---

[15] I have distinguished elsewhere between weak absoluteness and strong absoluteness (2014, 8–9; 2021, 2–3). A moral principle that is weakly absolute is binding always and everywhere. There are no exceptions to the bindingness of such a principle; there are no contexts in which its requirements are suspended or canceled. A moral principle that is strongly absolute is not only exceptionless – and is therefore not only weakly absolute – but is also always and everywhere more stringent than any other moral requirement(s) that might come into conflict with it. Here my assertion in the text about the absoluteness of many of the deontological duties engendered

I shall be charting some more in my forthcoming books on abortion and adjudicative procedures and distributive justice (*Abortion and the Limits of Governance*, *Shakespeare's Trials*, and *A Stoical Theory of Justice*).

Although the foci of those past and future books are multifarious, my ruminations therein converge on some key theses. I have applied two principal labels to those theses collectively: "Stoical liberalism" and "aspirational perfectionism." Instead of merging the two labels into a single cumbersome designation (as I have sometimes done), we are well advised to use them separately to denote distinctive strands of my theorizing about these matters.

The phrase "Stoical liberalism" captures well the ideal of self-restraint with which every system of governance is morally obligated to conform. As I have cautioned elsewhere (2021, 128), the adjective "Stoical" does not signal any allegiance to specific doctrines of ancient Hellenistic or Latin Stoicism. I pretermit and implicitly repudiate many prominent Stoical doctrines completely, and in my writings I do not grapple with all the philological and exegetical difficulties of pinning down what various ancient Stoical philosophers had in mind. Still, the inspiration for my political philosophy has been broadly Stoical, and readers familiar with the main ethical ideas of Hellenistic Stoicism will detect echoes of some of those ideas in my books which I have mentioned above. Although the echoes are somewhat tenuous, and although my publications in political philosophy stand or fall on their own merits rather than on the extent of their affinities with the outlooks and preoccupations of the Hellenistic Stoics, the connection to Stoicism draws attention to some of the central lines of reasoning in my reflections on how legal claim-rights and other legal entitlements should be distributed.

More specifically, Stoicism aptly associates an ideal of self-restraint with ethical strength. That is, a person or a system of governance comfortably capable of living up to the ideal of self-restraint is in that favorable position by dint of behaving or operating uprightly. A person or a system of governance not comfortably capable of living up to the ideal of self-restraint is in such an unfavorable position by dint of having already deviated from what is morally required. Hence, when a system of governance fails to abide by an ethic of self-restraint, its failure in that respect is both overweening and demeaning. Contraventions of such an ethic by such a system are obviously overweening in that they involve actions by the system that exceed the bounds of moral permissibility. Those actions might be meddlesome or high-handed or stiflingly restrictive, or they might partake of other vices that mark them out as grandiose and presumptuous. At the same time,

---

by the paramount moral responsibility of every system of governance is an ascription of weak absoluteness, rather than strong absoluteness, to those duties.

the actions that contravene the requirements of self-restraint are demeaning because they bespeak the inability or disinclination of the system of governance to fulfill other ethical requirements. A system that resorts to such overreaching is thereby engaging in self-condemnation through the very audacity of the over-reaching. The audacity is a manifestation – and, in effect, a proclamation – of the system's ethical weakness.

Let us glance at a couple of examples, to shed light on what has just been said. I have elsewhere pondered each of these examples at length. First, suppose that a governmental agency in charge of protecting public health is neglectful of its responsibilities and that it fails to undertake preparatory measures which could have averted a foreseeable outbreak of some disease (Kramer 2021, 146–147). When the highly transmissible disease consequently afflicts the community over which the regnant system of governance presides, the system's officials arrogate to themselves various legal and physical powers to control the details of the lives of individuals in order to stanch the outbreak. They prescribe how long individuals may remain away from home each day, and they sharply limit the number of people with whom any individual may fraternize. They issue decrees that legally prohibit restaurants and most shops (other than grocery shops) from operating, and they legally forbid activities such as theatrical productions and musical performances and religious services and museum exhibitions and athletic matches. These actions by the system of governance are blatantly overweening; they sweepingly steer the courses of people's lives by removing from individuals so many of the choices that are normally left uncurtailed in any society ruled by a system of governance that aspires to uphold the values of liberal democracy. In their overween-ingness, the edicts that proscribe a host of ordinary transactions and pastimes are also degrading, since they serve as the means of compensating for the remissness of the system of governance during the years when there were ample opportunities to head off any public-health emergency like the one that has now arisen. Those stifling edicts are thus the products of the failures by the system of governance to discharge its responsibilities. With the illiberality necessitated by such failures, the presiding system of governance both aggrandizes itself and demeans itself. It aggrandizes itself by exercising some extraordinary legal powers that impermissibly displace the decision-making latitude of individuals with the system's own determinations, and it debases itself because its having recourse to those powers is its means of coming to grips with the desperation that has been engendered by the system's own lackadaisicalness in the recent past.

For another familiar context in which the dynamic of overweeningness and demeaningness arises, we should contemplate the matter of hate-speech laws which I have elsewhere addressed in much greater depth.[16] Such laws are directed against the bigoted invective which hatemongers employ as they strive to induce their fellow citizens to abhor people from disfavored minority groups. Many instances of invective can be legally proscribed and penalized in consistency with the moral principle of freedom of expression, since many instances constitute communication-independent wrongdoing (to wit, wrongdoing that can be perpetrated either through communicative conduct or through non-communicative conduct). Hate-speech statutes are not needed for dealing with venomous utterances that are legitimately prohibitable on such grounds, since the venom can be handled perfectly well under laws that forbid the communication-independent types of wrongdoing which the specified utterances constitute. By contrast, vitriol that does not constitute any type of communication-independent wrongdoing is outside the reach of any of the laws that forbid such wrongdoing and is hence covered only by hate-speech statutes. In other words, the distinctive role of those statutes is to outlaw bigoted utterances that are not constitutive of any communication-independent misconduct.

However, when utterances are not constitutive of any serious communication-independent misconduct, the legal proscription of them is at odds with the moral principle of freedom of expression. Any subjection of those utterances to legal penalties would be morally impermissible not because stymieing the propagation of hatefulness is outside the proper sphere of any system of governance, but instead precisely because every such system is morally obligated to undertake numerous measures to counteract the ranting of bigots (and to counteract the noxious effects of the marketing of pornography). Numerous techniques that can and should be plied for that purpose by any system of governance are recounted in Chapters 5 and 6 of my 2021 book *Freedom of Expression as Self-Restraint*. Some of those techniques are anticipatory, whereas others are responsive to what has already occurred. Some are wide-ranging, whereas others are more narrowly focused. Diverse though the techniques are, however, they are alike in that they neither prohibit nor prevent any communicative activities that are not constitutive of communication-independent wrongdoing. Every system of governance is morally obligated to wield a large number of those sundry non-prohibitory and non-preventative methods for countering the spread of bigotry. In so doing, any such system will be endeavoring to fulfill its moral responsibility to foster and sustain a robust ethos of liberal democracy in its society, and it will thereby be acting in furtherance of the ideal of freedom of expression. That ideal is furthered by such methods partly because they are fully consistent with the requirements imposed by the moral principle of freedom of expression, but also (and even more) because

---

[16] See especially Chapters 4, 5, and 6 of Kramer (2021).

they obviate the need for any governmentally imposed restrictions that would be inconsistent with those requirements.

On the one hand, even in a society with a robust liberal-democratic ethos – cultivated by the techniques that have just been mentioned – some hatefully bigoted declamations will occur, and some pornographic films and magazines will continue to be manufactured and marketed. Such a society is not a fanciful utopia where the ugliness of those declamations and the dreariness of pornography have been entirely left behind. On the other hand, the sway of a robust liberal-democratic ethos in a society will have defused the effects of those noisome modes of communication. As I have argued at length in *Freedom of Expression as Self-Restraint*, the dominant effect of racist tirades in the presence of such an ethos is the discrediting of the people who deliver the tirades. Likewise, the marketing of pornographic materials in the presence of such an ethos will leave the political and economic and social standing of women unimpaired.

An ethos of the requisite kind, able to operate as an antidote to the poisonousness of these rebarbative modes of communication, is not something that can be taken for granted by any system of governance. On the contrary, it is something that has to be actively cultivated and upheld through governmental measures like those to which I have referred in the penultimate paragraph above. When a liberal-democratic ethos is properly nurtured and sustained, it endows a society with the ethical strength whereby a policy of toleration toward pornography and bigoted ranting – provided that the pornography or ranting does not amount to any communication-independent misconduct – is a way of reaffirming and reinforcing the potency of liberal-democratic values in the society. Directly relevant here is an insight voiced in Shakespeare's *Titus Andronicus* by Tamora, the former Queen of the Goths and now the wife of the Roman Emperor Saturninus, as she admonishes him that his prickly intolerance bespeaks weakness on his part (IV.iv.81–7):

> King, be thy thoughts imperious, like thy name.
> Is the sun dimm'd, that gnats do fly in it?
> The eagle suffers little birds to sing,
> And is not careful what they mean thereby,
> Knowing that with the shadow of his wings
> He can at pleasure stint their melody;
> Even so mayest thou the giddy men of Rome.

Tamora here discerns that unaccommodatingness or intolerance can often be a manifestation of weakness. She articulates that point predominantly with reference to the sheer physical might of the Roman Emperor as an autocrat, but her insight is even more pertinently applicable with reference to the ethical strength which a system of governance achieves through its cultivation and upholding of a robust societal ethos of liberal-democratic values. Like the eagle envisaged by Tamora that underscores its own pre-eminence and lofty assurance through its preparedness to let the little birds chirp, a system of governance that presides over the formation of a robust liberal-democratic ethos is sturdy enough to treat pornography and racist vitriol as chirping (when and only when the pornography or vitriol does not constitute any communication-independent misconduct).

Hence, when a system of governance seeks to outlaw pornographic materials or hateful diatribes that are not constitutive of any communication-independent wrongdoing, such a prohibition presupposes the failure of the system to bring about and solidify a robust ethos of the sort just outlined. For that system of governance, a prohibition along those lines is simultaneously an exercise in self-aggrandizement and an exercise in self-abasement. Its abasingness is evident from what has already been said here. A system of governance that has neglected to foster and preserve a strong societal ethos centered on the values of liberal democracy is thereby in contravention of its paramount moral responsibility – since the vibrant presence of such an ethos is integral to the political and social and economic conditions under which everyone in a society can be warranted in experiencing a hearty sense of self-respect. At least partly as a result of their failure to bring about such an ethos, the officials who run the system will need to quash modes of expression that would be tolerated (as worthless chirping) in a society with a proper level of ethical strength. Like an eagle that degradingly has to squelch the noises of feeble birds which it should be in a position to abide disdainfully, a system of governance demeans itself when its legal powers of prohibition and its physical powers of prevention are activated against modes of expression which it should be in a position to tolerate. Pornographic materials and racist fulminations that do not constitute any communication-independent wrongdoing are such modes of expression. Having to resort to legal bans or preventative measures in response to such materials and fulminations, a system of governance thereby implicitly avows the tenuousness of its achievements in any efforts by it to gain currency for the values of liberal democracy within the society over which it presides.

Even while a system of governance debases and implicitly condemns itself through the imposition of legal curbs on modes of expression that are not constitutive of any communication-independent misconduct, it likewise aggrandizes itself. The overweening directiveness of a system of governance as it outlaws those modes of expression is indisseverably connected to the ethical weakness of the system that stems from its failures to carry out the moral responsibilities which are incumbent upon it – most notably its moral obligation to promote and entrench an ethos of liberal-democratic values in its society. When a system of governance fulfills that ethos-cultivating obligation satisfactorily, the officials of the system are then comfortably in a position to comply with the moral duties imposed on them by the principle of freedom of expression. Securely in a position of ethical strength to uphold that moral principle, they can aptly treat the wares of pornographers and the maunderings of bigots as execrable chirps that are to be endured with contempt (again, when and only when the wares and maunderings are not rightly classifiable as communication-independent wrongdoing).

In short, the pattern of overweeningness and demeaningness which I have expounded is generated when a system of governance exercises its legal powers of proscription or its physical powers of prevention to suppress bigoted utterances that are not constitutive of communication-independent misconduct. Those exertions of powers by that system of governance are degrading – for the system itself and for the society over which it presides – because they presuppose the failure of the system to nurture and sustain a societal ethos that would serve as an antidote to the noxiousness of any bigoted rantings where those rantings do not constitute any communication-independent wrongdoing. That is, the exertions of powers presuppose the failure of the system to comply with its moral duty to bring about such an ethos, and they presuppose the failure of the citizenry to embrace such an ethos. The exertions of powers by the system of governance are likewise overweening, because through them the system's officials take control of communications that should have been countered and defused without interdictory or preventative impositions. The inordinate controllingness of the system ensues from its ethical weakness. In other words, because the system of governance has left itself and its society needlessly vulnerable to the baneful effects that can ultimately flow from certain types of communications where those effects have not been adequately warded off, the officials in the system feel obliged to offset their remissness with illiberality. Here as elsewhere, self-abasement and self-aggrandizement go hand in hand.

Because measures by a system of governance that contravene the moral principle of freedom of expression will detract from the moral integrity of the system in the ways that have been sketched here, they also detract from the levels of self-respect that are warranted for the members of the society over which the system presides. Here we shall encounter the strand of my Stoical liberalism that is best designated as "aspirational perfectionism." On the one hand, even were we to stay within the confines of Rawlsianism and Kantianism, we could descry some of the ways in which the measures that contravene the principle of freedom of expression impair the levels of self-respect that can warrantedly be harbored by the members of the society in which the measures are adopted. When legal-governmental officials close off the access of citizens to various ideas or sentiments conveyed by others – in circumstances where the conveyance of the ideas or sentiments is not correctly classifiable as communication-independent misconduct– they evince their distrust of the citizens' deliberative faculties. Instead of allowing sane adults to reach their own judgments about the ideas or sentiments in question, the officials lump those adults together with infants and lunatics as people from whom the latitude to arrive at such judgments is to be taken away. Being treated in such a disrespectful fashion, each sane adult is warranted in lowering his or her sense of self-respect. His or her life has been worsened through the subjection of him or her to such treatment.

Rawlsians and other Kantians are quite correct to complain about this aspect of the officials' actions. When a law forbids communicative activities that would not amount to any communication-independent wrongdoing, and when the rationale for such a ban is that the proscribed communications would insidiously deprave the outlooks of people through frequent exposure to those communications, adults of sound mind are indeed disrespectfully assimilated by such a law to gullible and irresponsible children. Sane adults treated so high-handedly are warranted in feeling aggrieved and would be unwarranted in reacting to the situation more favorably.

On the other hand, important though the concerns of Rawlsians and other Kantians are, the focus of the aspirational perfectionism in my Stoical liberalism lies predominantly on the relationship between any system of governance and the citizens who are ruled by the system. When such a system both aggrandizes itself and demeans itself through its adoption of laws or policies that bar the occurrence of certain modes of expression even though those modes of expression would not constitute any communication-independent misconduct, its tarnishing of its moral integrity in that manner negatively affects the level of self-respect that is warranted for each member of the relevant society. That negative impact occurs not only in the relatively straightforward way highlighted by the Rawlsians, but also in a more subtle and elaborate fashion highlighted by my aspirational perfectionism. As I have argued at length in *Liberalism with Excellence* (2017, 341–374), the doings of nearly every individual are located in matrices of social and economic and political relationships that bear crucially on the quality of his or her life. Those relationships will of course play major roles in determining whether the projects of any particular person eventuate in success or in frustration. However, in addition to the many direct influences exerted by the political and social and economic conditions wherein the life of anyone unfolds, an indirect influence is of distinctive importance that is charted throughout my expositions of aspirational perfectionism.

Each human being is warranted in gauging the quality of her life not only by reference to her own successes and failures but also by reference to the society (or societies) in which her life is embedded. As Chapter 8 of *Liberalism with Excellence* has maintained, the members of any society can warrantedly experience vicarious pride in its excellences and can warrantedly experience vicarious mortification over its shortcomings and misadventures. Associated as those members are with their society, they can be warranted in thinking that their own fortunes are to some degree bound up with its fortunes. At least insofar as the thriving of their society does not conflict with their own thriving, they can warrantedly feel that its thriving enhances their respective lives. Its flourishing elevates them. Because their identities have been formed in their society, and because they are identified therewith by other people, the flourishing of their society can make their own lives better – not only because it may improve their material prosperity but also because it can itself be a source of warranted pride for them as the society's members.

Now, as has been emphasized in *Liberalism with Excellence* (2017, 367–373), the premier form of thriving for any society is the sustainment of a liberal-democratic system of governance along with a corresponding ethos which pervades the society and which bolsters such a system. As has been detailed in that earlier book, the operations of the institutions which implement the requirements of justice in a liberal democracy are an outstanding collective accomplishment. Both on the part of legal-governmental officials and on the part of ordinary citizens, the patterns of self-restraint involved in the workings of just institutions are realistically achievable but immensely admirable. Every generally law-abiding person who belongs to a society ruled by a liberal-democratic system of governance can warrantedly take pride in the functioning of the system. Of course, in any actual liberal democracy – as opposed to the utopia of a well-ordered Rawlsian society – the operations of the prevailing institutions are imperfectly just, and the compliance of citizens with the just requirements laid down by those institutions is likewise imperfect. Nevertheless, in any society whose system of governance is liberal-democratic to a high degree and whose citizens embrace the values of liberal democracy to high degrees, the widespread adherence to those values is a mode of excellence in which every generally law-abiding citizen can warrantedly take pride. It is a mode of excellence that enhances the life of every generally law-abiding member of the society. In any actual liberal democracy, where citizens naturally tend to concentrate on the shortcomings of the established institutions, many of them sometimes lose sight of the preciousness and magnitude of the achievement that consists in the sustainment of those institutions. All the same, they can warrantedly derive satisfaction from that achievement – as the overall trajectory of the life of each generally law-abiding person P is made better by it. Because the course of P's life is inevitably affected (for better or for worse) by the tenor of the system of governance that presides over the society with which P is associated, the conformity of that system to the values of liberal democracy is something that heightens the level of self-respect which P can warrantedly harbor.

When I speak here about the heightening of the level of self-respect that is warranted for each generally law-abiding citizen, I am not proffering an empirical conjecture about the likelihood that each such citizen will be materially more affluent through the sway of a liberal-democratic system of governance in his or her society. On the one hand, there are quite strong and familiar correlations between liberal-democratic systems of governance and material prosperity. On the other hand, such correlations – important though they are – are not directly under consideration here. My contention about the shoring up of the level of self-respect which each generally law-abiding person can warrantedly harbor is focused on the inherent moral standing of liberal-democratic governance rather than on the beneficial consequences that are likely to ensue causally therefrom.

Rawls well captured two of the ways in which the inherent moral standing of liberal-democratic governance elevates the level of self-respect which each generally law-abiding member of a society can warrantedly feel. Throughout the long final chapter of *A Theory of Justice*, Rawls frequently declared that a liberal-democratic system of governance enables its citizens to realize their nature as free and equal persons. His pronouncements to that effect should be construed as making two main points. First, each person under a liberal-democratic system of governance is treated with the respect that befits a rationally deliberative agent who possesses both a sense of justice and a conception of what is valuable in life. Second, each person under such a system of governance is morally and legally required to exercise the self-restraint that shows due respect for other rationally deliberative agents. Being required to exercise such self-restraint is a hallmark of one's status as a free and equal person, as is being treated with commensurate forbearance by everybody else. Patterns of reciprocal temperance among citizens, and patterns of temperance by a system of governance in its interactions with citizens, encapsulate the status of every sane adult as a free and equal person. Rawls grasped and indeed stressed that those patterns of forbearance increase the level of self-esteem which a generally law-abiding person is warranted in experiencing. Having reminded his readers that his "account of [warranted] self-respect as perhaps the main primary good has stressed the great significance of how we think others value us," he proclaimed that a key "basis for [warranted] self-esteem in a just society is ... the publicly affirmed distribution of fundamental rights and liberties" (Rawls 1999, 477). He elaborated: "In a well-ordered society then [warranted] self-respect is secured [partly] by the public affirmation of the status of equal citizenship for all" (1999, 478). Of course, in addition to referring to the fundamental rights and liberties of citizenship, Rawls should have referred here to the fundamental responsibilities thereof. Each citizen's status as a free and equal person – along with the quantum of warranted self-respect which is appurtenant to that status – is upheld not only through her being endowed with the fundamental claim-rights and liberties, but also through her being expected and required to accept that each of her fellow citizens is correspondingly endowed with those claim-rights and liberties.

For a further crucial regard in which the sway of a liberal-democratic system of governance raises the level of self-respect that can warrantedly be harbored by each generally law-abiding person who lives under the jurisdiction of the system, we again need to go beyond Rawls and be guided by the aspirational perfectionism in my Stoical liberalism. As has already been remarked, the sustainment of a liberal democracy in any country – even with some imperfections – is a sterling collective achievement that should elicit feelings of pride on the part of everyone within that country whose conduct is generally lawful. Because the trajectory of the life of each generally law-abiding person there includes her association with a country in which that great collective accomplishment is occurrent, each such person can warrantedly believe that her life has gone better by virtue of the accomplishment (quite apart from any material wealth or other benefits that may have causally accrued to her as a result of it). *Pro tanto*, she can warrantedly feel better about herself and her projects than she otherwise could.

Conversely, of course, somebody who is a member of a society ruled by a repressively illiberal system of governance can warrantedly believe that her life has gone worse by dint of her links to that society (quite apart from any material hardships that may have beset her as a result of the system's grim oppression). Because the overall course of her life includes her connection to the country in which that system of governance reigns, it is marred by the fact that the people of the country – among them, most notably, the system's officials – have collectively failed to abide by the values of a liberal democracy. This point about the ethical worsening of a person's life is independent of her approval or disapproval of the tyrannical rulers. On the one hand, the trajectory of her life will be substantially worse ethically if she has been complicit in maintaining the grip of those rulers on power. On the other hand, my point here has not been about her personal responsibility for the persistence of the tyranny or for any of its iniquities; rather, this paragraph is about the collective responsibility of all the members of her community, with whom she is associated as a fellow member. Even if she has struggled gamely against the brutality of the system of governance in her country, her life that has been ennobled by the struggling is worsened ethically by the need for it – because the need for that struggling is due to a collective failure by a community to which she belongs.

Hence, when a system of governance contravenes the principle of freedom of expression – in deviations from self-restraint which, as such, are both presumptuous and ignominious for the system – it derogates from the level of self-respect that is warranted for each member of the society over which the system presides. Beyond any effect of reducing the opportunities for people to communicate their thoughts and sentiments, and beyond any effect of reducing the opportunities for people to gain acquaintance with the thoughts and sentiments articulated by others, the violations of the principle of freedom of expression sully the moral integrity of the system of governance that has perpetrated them. Because the benignity of the moral tenor of such a system in a society S should elicit pride among the members of S, and because the malignity of the moral tenor of such a system in a society T should elicit consternation among the members of T, the debasement of a system of governance through its contraventions of the principle of freedom of expression will have directly lowered the quantum of self-respect that is warranted for each member of the society over which the system presides. It directly diminishes the extent to which each of those members can warrantedly take pride in the prevailing system of governance as something with which each of them is associated. It diminishes the extent to which that system reflects well upon them. Consequently, any transgressions of the principle of freedom of expression by the officials in a system of governance are breaches of the system's paramount moral responsibility.

We have seen here in a nutshell how Stoical liberalism – with its aspirational-perfectionist attentiveness to the ways in which the members of any society Q should feel vicarious pride or vicarious shame with regard to the system of governance that rules Q – can serve to justify distributions of Hohfeldian legal positions that will tally with the principles of liberal democracy. Though we have just been contemplating the implications of Stoical liberalism for the communicative freedoms of people, there are far-reaching implications for countless other matters as well. As has been remarked, I have already brought to bear the insights of Stoical liberalism on debates over capital punishment and torture and public subsidies for the arts, and I shall be bringing those insights to bear on many more topics in the future (including the general topic of distributive justice). Hence, Stoical liberalism stands as a major alternative to Rawlsianism and Dworkinianism and other longstanding schools of thought within liberal political philosophy. It furnishes distinctive answers to questions about the extent to which and the ways in which the interests of various beings should be legally protected, and it is likewise distinctive in its identification of the moral principles that undergird the answers to those questions.

## 4 A Laconic Conclusion

In a very short compass, this Elements volume has covered a wide range of issues pertaining to rights and the holding of rights. It has addressed an array of non-justificatory questions about the nature of claim-rights and other Hohfeldian entitlements (and their correlative positions), and it has tackled some additional non-justificatory questions about the conditions necessary and sufficient for the holding of claim-rights and other entitlements. Broaching yet another set of non-justificatory questions, this volume has pondered what sorts of beings can hold claim-rights at all. After exploring those non-justificatory matters, I have proceeded to draw attention to an array of justificatory topics and considerations that bear on how the interests of various parties should be protected through the bestowal of legal entitlements. Having opposed the constructivism of Rawls and the ostensible methodological austerity of Steiner, the volume has concluded by examining a quite recent alternative to the accounts of justice that prevailed in twentieth-century liberalism. On every topic with which I have engaged here, much more remains to be said – and much more has been said in other books and essays. Readers are heartily encouraged to pursue these matters further in the texts of contemporary legal philosophy and political philosophy.

# References

Anderson, Elizabeth. 1999. "What Is the Point of Equality?" 109 *Ethics* 287–337.

Barkham, Patrick. 2021. "Should Rivers Have the Same Rights as People?" *The Observer*, July 25. www.theguardian.com/environment/2021/jul/25/rivers-around-the-world-rivers-are-gaining-the-same-legal-rights-as-people.

Campbell, Tom. 2001. *Justice*. 2nd ed. Basingstoke: Macmillan Press.

Carter, Ian. 1999. *A Measure of Freedom*. Oxford: Oxford University Press.

Cohen, G. A. 2008. *Rescuing Justice and Equality*. Cambridge, MA: Harvard University Press.

Cruft, Rowan. 2019. *Human Rights, Ownership, and the Individual*. Oxford: Oxford University Press.

Dworkin, Ronald. 1978. *Taking Rights Seriously*. Cambridge, MA: Harvard University Press.

Dworkin, Ronald. 1986. *Law's Empire*. London: Fontana Press.

Dworkin, Ronald. 2000. *Sovereign Virtue*. Cambridge, MA: Harvard University Press.

Dworkin, Ronald. 2011. *Justice for Hedgehogs*. Cambridge, MA: Harvard University Press.

Frankfurt, Harry. 2015. *On Inequality*. Princeton, NJ: Princeton University Press.

Freeman, Samuel. 2007. *Justice and the Social Contract*. Oxford: Oxford University Press.

Gauthier, David. 1986. *Morals by Agreement*. Oxford: Oxford University Press.

Gilbert, Margaret. 2018. *Rights and Demands*. Oxford: Oxford University Press.

Hart, H. L. A. 1982. *Essays on Bentham*. Oxford: Oxford University Press.

Hart, H. L. A. 1994. *The Concept of Law*. 2nd ed. Oxford: Oxford University Press.

Kramer, Matthew. 2009a. "Consistency Is Hardly Ever Enough: Reflections on Hillel Steiner's Methodology." In Stephen de Wijze, Matthew Kramer, and Ian Carter (eds), *Hillel Steiner and the Anatomy of Justice*. New York: Routledge, pp. 201–213.

Kramer, Matthew. 2009b. *Moral Realism as a Moral Doctrine*. Oxford: Wiley-Blackwell.

Kramer, Matthew. 2011. *The Ethics of Capital Punishment*. Oxford: Oxford University Press.

Kramer, Matthew. 2014. *Torture and Moral Integrity*. Oxford: Oxford University Press.

Kramer, Matthew. 2017. *Liberalism with Excellence*. Oxford: Oxford University Press.

Kramer, Matthew. 2018. *H. L. A. Hart: The Nature of Law*. Cambridge: Polity Press.

Kramer, Matthew. 2021. *Freedom of Expression as Self-Restraint*. Oxford: Oxford University Press.

Kramer, Matthew. 2024. *Rights and Right-Holding*. Oxford: Oxford University Press.

Kramer, Matthew and Steiner, Hillel. 2007. "Theories of Rights: Is There a Third Way?" 27 *Oxford Journal of Legal Studies* 281–310.

Kurki, Visa. 2019. *A Theory of Legal Personhood*. Oxford: Oxford University Press.

Kurki, Visa. 2022. "Can Nature Hold Rights? It's Not as Easy as You Think." 11 *Transnational Environmental Law* 525–552.

MacCormick, Neil. 1977. "Rights in Legislation." In Peter Hacker and Joseph Raz (eds), *Law, Morality, and Society*. Oxford: Oxford University Press, pp. 189–209.

McBride, Mark. 2022. "Tracking the Resilience of Hybridity." In Mark McBride and Visa Kurki (eds), *Without Trimmings: The Legal, Moral, and Political Philosophy of Matthew Kramer*. Oxford: Oxford University Press, pp. 93–110.

Miller, David. 1999. *Principles of Social Justice*. Cambridge, MA: Harvard University Press.

Mills, Charles. 1997. *The Racial Contract*. Ithaca, NY: Cornell University Press.

Nozick, Robert. 1974. *Anarchy, State, and Utopia*. New York, NY: Basic Books.

Nussbaum, Martha. 2006. *Frontiers of Justice*. Cambridge, MA: Harvard University Press.

Okin, Susan Moller. 1989. *Justice, Gender, and the Family*. New York, NY: Basic Books.

Rawls, John. 1971. *A Theory of Justice*. Cambridge, MA: Harvard University Press.

Rawls, John. 1974. "The Independence of Moral Theory." 47 *Proceedings and Addresses of the American Philosophical Association* 5–22.

Rawls, John. 1993. *Political Liberalism*. New York, NY: Columbia University Press.

Rawls, John. 1999. *A Theory of Justice*. Revised ed. Oxford: Oxford University Press.

Raz, Joseph. 1986. *The Morality of Freedom*. Oxford: Oxford University Press.

Scanlon, Thomas. 1998. *What We Owe to Each Other*. Cambridge, MA: Harvard University Press.

Sen, Amartya. 2009. *The Idea of Justice*. Cambridge, MA: Harvard University Press.

Simmonds, N. E. 1998. "Rights at the Cutting Edge." In Matthew Kramer, N. E. Simmonds, and Hillel Steiner (eds), *A Debate over Rights*. Oxford: Oxford University Press, pp. 113–232.

Sreenivasan, Gopal. 2005. "A Hybrid Theory of Claim-Rights." 25 *Oxford Journal of Legal Studies* 257–274.

Sreenivasan, Gopal. 2010. "Duties and Their Direction." 120 *Ethics* 465–494.

Steiner, Hillel. 1994. *An Essay on Rights*. Oxford: Blackwell.

Steiner, Hillel. 1998. "Working Rights." In Matthew Kramer, N. E. Simmonds, and Hillel Steiner (eds), *A Debate over Rights*. Oxford: Oxford University Press, pp. 233–301.

Stockwell, Billy. 2022. "The Rights of Rivers." *The Ecologist*, August 9. https://theecologist.org/2022/aug/09/rights-rivers.

Stone, Christopher. 1972. "Should Trees Have Standing? – Toward Legal Rights for Natural Objects." 45 *Southern California Law Review* 450–501.

Young, Iris Marion. 1990. *Justice and the Politics of Difference*. Princeton, NJ: Princeton University Press.

# Acknowledgments

I am grateful to Kenneth Ehrenberg for his suggestions and to an anonymous reader for some valuable comments that prompted me to undertake several salutary amplifications.

Cambridge Elements ☰

# Philosophy of Law

## Series Editors

### George Pavlakos
*University of Glasgow*

George Pavlakos is Professor of Law and Philosophy at the School of Law, University of Glasgow. He has held visiting posts at the universities of Kiel and Luzern, the European University Institute, the UCLA Law School, the Cornell Law School and the Beihang Law School in Beijing. He is the author of *Our Knowledge of the Law* (2007) and more recently has co-edited *Agency, Negligence and Responsibility* (2021) and *Reasons and Intentions in Law and Practical Agency* (2015).

### Gerald J. Postema
*University of North Carolina at Chapel Hill*

Gerald J. Postema is Professor Emeritus of Philosophy at the University of North Carolina at Chapel Hill. Among his publications count *Utility, Publicity, and Law: Bentham's Moral and Legal Philosophy* (2019); *On the Law of Nature, Reason, and the Common Law: Selected Jurisprudential Writings of Sir Matthew Hale* (2017); *Legal Philosophy in the Twentieth Century: The Common Law World* (2011), *Bentham and the Common Law Tradition*, 2nd edition (2019).

### Kenneth M. Ehrenberg
*University of Surrey*

Kenneth M. Ehrenberg is Professor of Jurisprudence and Philosophy at the University of Surrey School of Law and Co-Director of the Surrey Centre for Law and Philosophy. He is the author of *The Functions of Law* (2016) and numerous articles on the nature of law, jurisprudential methodology, the relation of law to morality, practical authority, and the epistemology of evidence law.

## Associate Editor

### Sally Zhu
*University of Sheffield*

Sally Zhu is a Lecturer in Property Law at University of Sheffield. Her research is on property and private law aspects of platform and digital economies.

## About the Series

This series provides an accessible overview of the philosophy of law, drawing on its varied intellectual traditions in order to showcase the interdisciplinary dimensions of jurisprudential enquiry, review the state of the art in the field, and suggest fresh research agendas for the future. Focussing on issues rather than traditions or authors, each contribution seeks to deepen our understanding of the foundations of the law, ultimately with a view to offering practical insights into some of the major challenges of our age.

Cambridge Elements ≡

# Philosophy of Law

Printed in the United States
by Baker & Taylor Publisher Services